I0166536

The Haitian Revolution

An Enthralling Tale of Resistance, Freedom, and the Birth of a Nation

© Copyright 2024 - All rights reserved.

The content contained within this book may not be reproduced, duplicated, or transmitted without direct written permission from the author or the publisher.

Under no circumstances will any blame or legal responsibility be held against the publisher, or author, for any damages, reparation, or monetary loss due to the information contained within this book, either directly or indirectly.

Legal Notice:

This book is copyright protected. It is only for personal use. You cannot amend, distribute, sell, use, quote, or paraphrase any part, or the content within this book, without the consent of the author or publisher.

Disclaimer Notice:

Please note the information contained within this document is for educational and entertainment purposes only. All effort has been executed to present accurate, up-to-date, reliable, and complete information. No warranties of any kind are declared or implied. Readers acknowledge that the author is not engaging in the rendering of legal, financial, medical, or professional advice. The content within this book has been derived from various sources. Please consult a licensed professional before attempting any techniques outlined in this book.

By reading this document, the reader agrees that under no circumstances is the author responsible for any losses, direct or indirect, that are incurred as a result of the use of the information contained within this document, including, but not limited to, errors, omissions, or inaccuracies.

Free limited time bonus

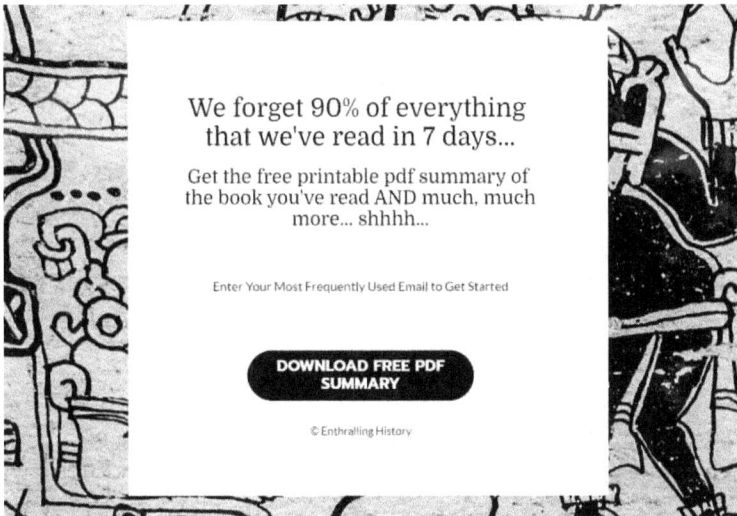

We forget 90% of everything
that we've read in 7 days...

Get the free printable pdf summary of
the book you've read AND much, much
more... shhhh...

Enter Your Most Frequently Used Email to Get Started

**DOWNLOAD FREE PDF
SUMMARY**

© Enthralling History

Stop for a moment. We have a free bonus set up for you. The problem is this: we forget 90% of everything that we read after 7 days. Crazy fact, right? Here's the solution: we've created a printable, 1-page pdf summary for this book that you're reading now. All you have to do to get your free pdf summary is to go to the following website: **https://livetolearn.lpages.co/enthrallinghistory/**

Or, Scan the QR code!

Once you do, it will be intuitive. Enjoy, and thank you!

Table of Contents

Introduction

The Haitian Revolution, which began in August of 1791 in the French Caribbean colony of Saint-Domingue, has cemented itself as one of the most compelling emancipatory conflicts in early modern history. As a profoundly anti-white insurrection launched by the black slave population on the island, it eventually became one of the most iconic of such movements. Of course, a significant aspect behind this was its successful outcome for the revolutionaries, ending in the new Republic of Haiti's proclamation of independence on January 1, 1804.

Historians rightfully hail the importance of the Haitian Revolution, inspired by the American Revolution, which had been completed in 1783, and the turbulency of the French Revolution, which had begun just two years prior, in 1789, Indeed, the three movements are often grouped under the umbrella of the "Atlantic Revolutions," emphasizing similarities that run deep. Taken independently and together, these movements shaped the socio-political and cultural landscapes of their nations and regions, with widespread influences that molded the rest of the history of the nineteenth century and beyond.

Still, the Haitian Revolution often gets overshadowed by the American and French revolutions, perhaps because their impact on world history was felt more directly and clearly than Haiti's.

However, at the end of the eighteenth century, the island of Hispaniola, where the French colony of Saint-Domingue was located, was one of the most valuable colonial territories. About a hundred years after its acquisition from Spain by France in 1697, Saint-Domingue had the largest and fastest-growing African slave market in the Western Hemisphere, even bigger than that of the United States. Tens of thousands of black slaves imported every year from Africa were dispersed in the hundreds of coffee, sugar, cotton, and indigo plantations in the colony, where they worked relentlessly for their white masters. These products were among the most valuable in the world, primarily due to their excessive consumption by European markets, making Saint-Domingue an especially profitable colony for France.

The Haitian Revolution itself had immediate consequences, partly because it was a defeat of mighty France, whose strength had reached its peak under Emperor Napoleon Bonaparte. For example, it prompted the United States' purchase of the huge North American colony of Louisiana from France, which greatly accelerated American westward expansion and its transformation into first a regional and then a global superpower. The failure of the French forces to subdue the insurrection in Saint-Domingue can also be seen as a preview of what would come when France was confronted with unorthodox fighting strategies in other theaters of war, such as Spain and Russia, a few years later. Moreover, the forced migration of former white colonists into the US from Haiti also resulted in their settling in the now-American city of New Orleans, which eventually became the largest city of the American South. The cultural influences of this migration can still be observed.

The outcome of the Haitian Revolution can also be observed as having a profound influence on the nineteenth-century colonial struggles in the Western Hemisphere, which we will cover in great detail in later chapters.

In short, perhaps yes, the Haitian Revolution is the youngest brother of the Atlantic Revolutions. But its effects, though sometimes overshadowed by the American and French revolutions, deserve the attention of scholars and curious minds that want to explore its exciting details.

Interestingly, the term "Haitian Revolution" refers to a pair of contemporary and largely disconnected movements and is one of the reasons it constitutes a unique development from the American and French cases. The slave uprising, which began in August 1791 and is considered the beginning of the Haitian Revolution, was a regional phenomenon, affecting just one out of the three provinces of Saint-Domingue. Alongside it was a movement of the free black people of the colony, whose goals and actions did not necessarily correspond with those of the enslaved until the late stages of the revolution. This disconnection between the two movements would continue even after the proclamation of independence in 1804. Soon after, the Republic of Haiti split into two rival states in a struggle that would last until 1820.

It is also important to realize that the Haitian Revolution was driven primarily by the illiterate population of the colony. This means we know about the events of the Haitian Revolution, including its ill-defined goals, from outsider sources, most of whom were quite hostile to the whole insurrection. Identification of the "leader" of the revolution also becomes a problem because of this, as the man to whom this role is attributed, Toussaint Louverture, was not always actively involved in the movement. In fact, he played a dubious part in most of it. He was not in favor of the complete abolition of slavery despite being a black man, switched from fighting against the French to fighting for them, and used the power he acquired from his leadership of the revolutionary army to push for some very conservative measures that were not endorsed by the black population of the colony.

The uniqueness of the Haitian Revolution, relative to the American and French ones, stems exactly from these reasons. But this should not be a reason to undermine its absolute significance and widespread influences, whether hidden and long-term or strongly felt and immediate. The aim of this book is thus to tell the enthralling history of the Haitian Revolution, not only examining the events of 1791 to 1804 but also diving deep into its root causes and consequences. From the inspiring actions of the revolutionaries and their compelling social and cultural dynamics to the bloody massacres and relentless military engagements that determined the outcome of the conflict, there is certainly a lot to unpack in the Haitian Revolution.

Chapter One – The Shadows of Slavery: Pre-Revolution

In the opening chapter, we will explore the French colony of Saint-Domingue before the uprisings in 1791 that would eventually mark the beginning of the Haitian Revolution. Saint-Domingue, located on the western part of the island of Hispaniola, was referred to as the "Pearl of the Antilles" because of its immense economic importance as a colony for France. Despite its size in comparison to the neighboring colonial possessions of other European powers, Saint-Domingue was the single most profitable colony in 1791. The economic output of the colony was only possible because of the disproportionately large black slave population of Saint-Domingue, which was subject to harsh living and working conditions. Below, we will dive deep into the details of the French colony and examine the circumstances present there before the Haitian Revolution.

French Saint-Domingue

The island of Hispaniola in the Caribbean holds a special place in world history—it is the island where Christopher Columbus and his expedition first landed in 1492. There, Columbus and his crew encountered the local Taino peoples, who were, as everyone knows, not the same "Indians" the expedition had originally set out to reach. Nevertheless, the Spanish soon began to colonize the island, giving it its name and establishing the first settlements that would eventually turn Hispaniola into a focal point of Spanish colonial activities in the

Americas. It became a safe stop the Spanish colonists would reach to continue their journeys into the unexplored continental lands of the Americas, which promised much more riches and glory than Hispaniola.

The town of Santo Domingo, founded in 1496 on the west bank of the Ozana River in the southeastern part of the colony and now the capital city of the modern Dominican Republic, became an important site of the expanding Spanish colonial enterprise. It was built up not only as a connecting hub between the Americas and Europe but also as a defensive center against Spain's European rivals that soon followed in its footsteps to take over the New World themselves.

One such rival was France, which founded its first colonial settlement in 1626 on the smaller Caribbean island of Saint-Christophe (now Saint Kitts). The French also took the islands of Guadalupe and Martinique and established their presence in Canada. In addition to these territories, independent groups of sailors would settle unexplored territories in the New World and claim them for themselves or their nations. These groups, known as buccaneers, were common at the time, as the exploration of the New World was ongoing and contact between mainland Europe and the Americas took months.

A group of French buccaneers thus settled in the northern part of Hispaniola sometime in the seventeenth century, and the French government appointed a governor for the colony in the 1660s. What followed in Europe was a large-scale escalation between France and an alliance of European powers that included Spain. Known as the Nine Years' War, it ended with the Peace of Ryswick in 1697. A portion of the complicated peace agreement was Spain's cession of the western part of the island of Hispaniola to France, thus formalizing the possessions claimed by the French buccaneers decades before the conflict. In addition to an array of other territorial changes both in Europe and in the colonies, the Nine Years' War thus resulted in France possessing the part of Hispaniola that became the French colony of Saint-Domingue—the colony that would revolt a century later against the Crown.

The French colonial enterprise soon realized the potential of Saint-Domingue and transformed the largely unsettled part of the island into a lucrative colony. The administration of the colony was divided into north, west, and south provinces, and each province had a specialization. Northern Saint-Domingue became a center of growing sugar (one of the most in-demand products at the time) because of its flat plains that were perfect for the plant. The hillier western province began producing coffee, another massively popular product for Europe in the seventeenth century. Coffee could be grown on the uneven terrain of the island's western territories much easier than sugar, and the plantations, were generally cheaper to set up, needing less maintenance. The southern province, which was settled later, could not boast about its agricultural output compared to the other provinces, but its ports engaged in heavy trade with Spanish, Dutch, and English colonies. Cotton and indigo were the other two commodities produced in the colony, though it was coffee and sugar that made the French the most money from Saint-Domingue.

Thanks to a perfect climate and the profitable nature of these goods, French Saint-Domingue became the most valuable colony of France and one of the most valuable in the New World. By the mid-eighteenth century, it had a thriving economy, with thousands of plantations that produced more than about seventy million pounds of sugar and fifty-five million pounds of coffee alone. To put it into perspective, the growth meant that the colony exported about half of all the sugar and coffee consumed by Europe and the colonies by 1789.

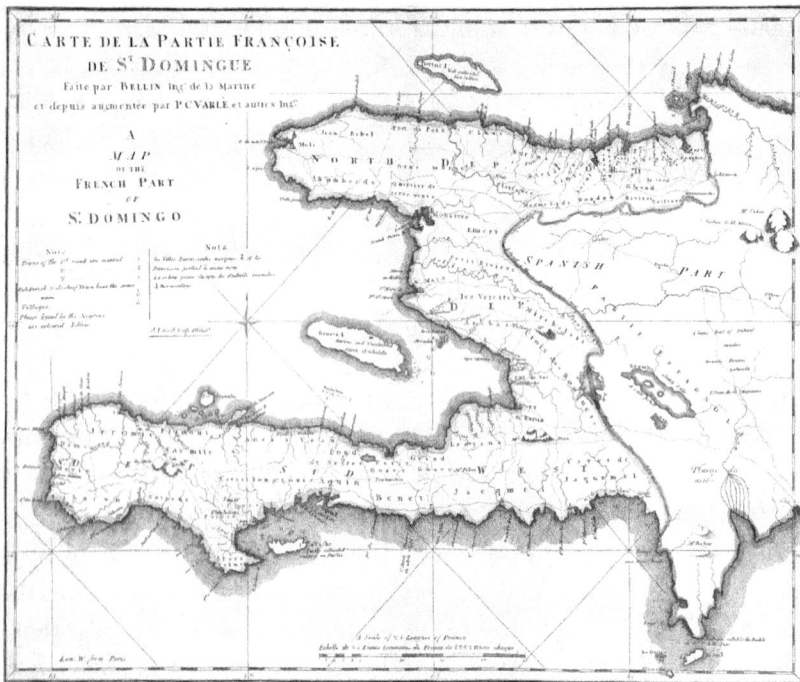

Map of French Saint-Domingue from 1789.
https://commons.wikimedia.org/wiki/File:SaintDomingue.360.jpg

Such rapid transformation of Saint-Domingue created a demand for labor in the colony. The French Crown profited immensely from taxing Saint-Domingue and allowed the establishment of an equally extensive slave network in the colony. In the eighteenth century, France was one of the beneficiaries of the Atlantic slave trade network. French ships, full of manufactured goods like textiles and guns, would trade with native African states for local slaves, both men and women. Transported by overcrowded vessels, on which as many as one sixth of all slaves died before even crossing the Atlantic, the enslaved reached Saint-Domingue. There, they would be sold on local markets to plantation owners to be brutally exploited all their lives. The Atlantic slave trade was a complicated and carefully-planned network that cost the lives of millions and transformed the demographic landscape of the world. In Saint-Domingue alone, the number of black slaves grew exponentially, from just over 3,300 in 1687 to nearly 250,000 by the end of the 1770s. In comparison, the white population of the colony in 1779 was about 32,600 people.

Society of Saint-Domingue

Black slaves thus made up the overwhelming majority of the population in Saint-Domingue. Most of them did not live in cities but in the countryside on the private plantations of wealthy French planters. Such a high slave population meant that there were clearcut differences between classes of slaves based on the nature of their labor, their gender, and even their relationship to their masters. Male and female slaves had different jobs on the plantation, for example. Males did the labor that required more physical strength and skill, such as carrying out the processes that transformed harvested sugar canes into sugar. Female slaves, on the other hand, did most of the field work, such as planting and harvesting. Slaves usually worked in groups and youngsters were assigned to them to pick up the skills necessary for the different types of labor. In addition to field slaves, who were the lowest in the hierarchy, there were also domestic slaves used for house activities.

Some were higher in the hierarchy than others. The job of the *commandeur*, for example, was to oversee the activities of other slaves, directly reporting to their masters. The *commandeurs* had closer relationships with their white owners, who, in return for loyalty, also treated them with respect. They were sometimes exempted from doing harsh manual labor and given separate lodgings and a simple education.

It is rather difficult for someone today to fully imagine the extent of the exploitation of black slaves that worked on plantations in the eighteenth century. Work on coffee and sugar plantations was very difficult and required precision and skill. Sugar canes, harvested from the end of January until July each year, had to be instantly processed before they lost their sweetness. Their juice had to be boiled in large cauldrons and then poured into molds for sugar to achieve a crystalized form. This meant that most slaves worked throughout the day and night, with many dying from exhaustion.

In addition to their work, slaves were also in charge of small private land plots where they harvested food for themselves. Keeping a balance between the maintenance of their meager gardens and exhausting labor was very difficult, resulting in malnutrition, chiefly due to a lack of meat in their diets. Often, they had to live in large shared spaces, which meant a lack of privacy and low levels of sanitation, another major cause of death. Upon being brought from Africa to the Caribbean, many slaves contracted fatal diseases and illnesses, partially due to sanitation problems and partially due to the differences in climate conditions.

Overall, when combined with the psychological trauma that accompanied exploitation, the physical hardships encountered by black slaves resulted in very high mortality rates among them. Most died within seven to ten years of being brought to the colonies, while about a third died during their first year. For the white colonists, this meant nothing more than an ever-increasing demand for new slaves to replace the workforce that would frequently perish.

Technically, the legal basis for slavery in France was provided by the "Code Noir," a codex issued in 1685 that made slavery legal in the colonies. The code dictated the general regulations for the treatment of the slaves, but these regulations were rarely, if at all, enforced. For instance, slaveowners had to provide slaves with adequate daily food rations, annual sets of clothing, and a rest day each week. In practice, most slaves were underfed and wore rags. This is not to speak of the harsh punishments they would incur regularly for various reasons. They were routinely whipped and maimed. Some were thrown into small compartments on the plantations that served as prison punishment for disobedience. Slaves would be kept in these compartments without food for days, sometimes in complete darkness. The harshest punishments were for those who had tried to escape but were caught. Slaveowners often made an example out of such slaves in front of others to install fear. They branded the slaves with different marks to identify that they had been former escapees and shackled them with iron collars.

Though the Code Noir also gave slaves the right to appeal to authorities about their mistreatment, this was rarely allowed, and their sentiments were simply ignored. Either way, only a minority of slaves were literate or spoke French. Newly-arrived slaves, referred to as *Bossales,* would pick up the Creole language, a combination of French and local African tongues that the slaves used to communicate among themselves. African-born *Bossales* were considered harder to manage than *Creoles* born into slavery in the colonies, so more attention was devoted to them upon their arrival.

In Saint-Domingue, just as everywhere else where black people were enslaved, the outnumbered white population of the island kept its power by constant intimidation and force. The 30,000 or so white people who lived in the French colony were only supported by a small army garrison but maintained order in society relatively well until 1791.

On paper, of course, had most of the slaves united, they could have easily won their freedom by overpowering the white population. But the slaves in Saint-Domingue hardly had a developed sense of community and brotherhood, as all their efforts were constantly undermined by the colonists. Nevertheless, they managed to develop some unique ways of communal life, gathering on their off days and engaging in ceremonies and rituals that mixed traditional African and Christian elements. The vibrant vodou religion is a prominent example. In vodou dance rituals, worshippers enter trance-like states full of ecstasy, during which their spirits contact various African spirits. The African spirits, called *lwa,* came to represent Catholic saints in vodou practices due to the Christian influences the black slaves had adopted from their masters. The vodou religion became the most prominent form of spiritual self-expression for slaves that were deprived of all other social and cultural life. Slaveowners, though aware of the vodou ceremonies that would sometimes take place on their plantations, chose to leave the slaves alone in those instances, perhaps fearing that a complete suppression of their community was not a wise move.

In addition to white slaveowners and black slaves, a third social category developed over time in French Saint-Domingue: free people of color. Free people of color were former black slaves who had managed to ascend all the way up the slave hierarchy and achieve freedom by hiring themselves out from their masters. Usually, this only happened to slaves who dwelled with their masters in urban areas and possessed a useful skill, such as artisanship. The instances of white slaveowners freeing their slaves were rare and required slaves to put in years of dedicated work and discipline.

In addition, a portion of this group was made up of the offspring of white colonists and black slave women. Sexual exploitation of women slaves was a common practice among the colonists, partly because there were fewer white women in the colonies. (Women were less reluctant than men to leave Europe in search of new lives.) White men would thus often free their black slave concubines and their children. There were instances where newly freed slaves would inherit possessions from their white fathers—including slaves.

As time passed and the number of free people of color increased in Saint-Domingue, this racial group began to identify itself more with the white population of the island than the slaves. They built up their private possessions, worked regular jobs, and mostly lived in the cities. The census of 1789 showed that there were about 28,000 free people of color in Saint-Domingue—almost as many as the white population of the island. However, this also meant that they demanded more rights and equal treatment from whites, who had always been wary of them.

Though the Code Noir had specified that free people of color were to be treated as equals, in practice, this was not the case. By the second half of the eighteenth century, the white population was pushing for more laws to limit the freedoms of free people of color and highlight the differences among them to dissuade further demands for equality. Thus, free people of color were excluded from certain jobs, such as practicing medicine or law, and from occupying positions in government or military command. The outbreak of the French Revolution in 1789 nevertheless pushed the free people of color to begin their movement for equality, which eventually fueled the Haitian Revolution and developed parallel to the slave revolt two years later.

This is not to say there weren't obvious social distinctions between the whites in Saint-Domingue. These distinctions were noted even by the blacks, who called the less successful colonists *petit blancs*, or "little whites," and more successful ones *grand blancs* ("great whites"). *Petit blancs* were only higher in the social hierarchy than black people due to their skin color. They were colonists who had failed to find the fortune they had hoped for. In contrast, *grand blancs* were the real deal in Saint-Domingue. Many of them had been the early benefactors of the sugar and coffee plantations, which had allowed them to increase their possessions to astronomical levels.

By the time of the Haitian Revolution, the richest of the colonists lived in lavish houses in plantations that spanned acres of land—houses decorated with expensive furniture imported from Europe. The plantation owners were, in many instances, as rich as members of the French bourgeoisie. The chief difference was that the colonists hated the mainland government, which they thought, due to jealousy, wanted to exploit their riches by heavy taxation. By and large, this was not far from reality. French officials were perfectly aware of the magnitude of the riches that flowed into the country from the colonies. The government had, in fact, passed a law that required the French colonists to exclusively buy from French merchants. This meant the merchants could overcharge them when selling manufactured European goods and undercharge them when buying the coffee and sugar produced by the colonists. This is why the Southern province of Saint-Domingue eventually came to specialize in contraband trade with English, Spanish, and Dutch merchants, bypassing the laws enforced from the motherland.

The *grand blancs* possessed an enormous influence in the colony and detested efforts to keep their lives in check, such as when officials from the mainland were appointed to important administrative roles. This was despite the fact that they fully considered themselves members of the high echelons of society in France.

The colonists imitated everything they could from their motherland, as was the common practice in the New World at the time. Cap Français, the main city in Saint-Domingue located on the northern coast, was a full-fledged European city. Commonly called Le Cap, it had a carefully planned rectangular grid and a population of about 18,000 people. Its inhabitants enjoyed the bustling cafes, theaters, and salons as other French did, and tried to keep up with the mode of living in the motherland. Le Cap was an example of a typical French city during the Enlightenment era. It was larger and richer than the official capital of the colony, Port-au-Prince, which was located in the West and could not boast paved streets and stone buildings as Le Cap could.

Saint-Domingue and the French Revolution

As mentioned, the white society of Saint-Domingue considered themselves—and were, in most aspects—full-fledged Europeans. They spoke, dressed, and lived like their counterparts from the motherland in cities that resembled those of the motherland. Often, they were far richer—the main reason behind their constant desire for more self-governance without necessarily cutting all ties with France.

This constant rivalry between the *grand blancs* of the colony and the French administration continued throughout the second half of the eighteenth century and reached its zenith in 1783, after the end of the American War of Independence. This war saw the Thirteen Colonies, previously under the control of Great Britain, become the sovereign United States of America.

The emergence of such a close neighbor spelled the beginning of new trade relations between Saint-Domingue and the Americans, which opposed the interests of the French merchants who nominally held exclusive rights to trade in Saint-Domingue. As a response to the opening of trade, the French government issued new regulations regarding the slavery system in the years following 1783. In hindsight, these regulations were nothing too severe, requiring things like keeping track of food rations and clothing that should have been given to the slaves. However, the white slaveowners of Saint-Domingue were outraged, believing that the new measures were directed to unjustly punish them and could threaten their economic and social security.

The tensions escalated further after 1788, as France was enchanted by the revolutionary spirit. The truth was that France was in a deep economic crisis, something that was felt the most by the lowest echelons of French society. The Estates General—an ancient institution that represented the interests of the different classes of the clergy, nobility, and commoners—was summoned by King Louis XVI to discuss the ongoing situation and come up with a solution fit for everyone.

At the assembly in June 1789, however, the Third Estate, comprised of French peasants and bourgeoisie who had felt the toll of the crisis the most and represented most of the population, was overpowered by the First and the Second Estates. This was because each received one vote with equal power, and the clergy and the nobility had common interests, leading them to work together to implement measures favorable for them. The outraged members of the Third Estate thus took a radical step, challenging the authority of the king and the other classes and declaring themselves the National Assembly, kicking off the French Revolution. On July 14, 1789, motivated by a republican spirit, they stormed the Bastille Prison in Paris, a symbol of the despotism of the old regime.

The events of the French Revolution had ripple effects all over the world, including in the colony of Saint-Domingue, where it took weeks for the information from Paris to arrive. Representatives of the colonists of Saint-Domingue in Paris who had witnessed the insurrection of the Third Estate supported the movement. They believed they had the right to adequate representation in French governmental affairs based on the economic importance of Saint-Domingue and its adverse relationship with the administration in France. The National Assembly welcomed Saint-Domingue, giving the colony six seats in the new representative government it aimed to create, despite the fact that many of its members opposed slavery as a practice. The colonists were hopeful that the assembly, which was still fighting for dominance with the royalists in the country, would not adopt measures that might endanger the status quo in the colonies. However, with the adoption of the Declaration of the Rights of Man and of the Citizen by the National Assembly in August, they became increasingly wary.

The declaration asserted universal human rights, with its very first article famously claiming that "men are born and remain free and equal in rights." It is not difficult to guess why the colonists in Saint-Domingue were not on board. The National Assembly had aimed to abolish all social hierarchy in France in favor of the total equality and liberty of all individuals, but it had been started primarily by the peasantry of France, who did not see the exploitation of black slaves as a valid practice. The declaration thus raised questions about the practice of slavery in the colonies, something the National Assembly chose to ignore to deal with "more urgent" matters in the homeland.

The authorities in Saint-Domingue, carefully following the unfolding situation in Paris, decided to prohibit the circulation of French newspapers in the colony, afraid that the ideas of the revolution might lead to problems. They were right. In August, there was a slave uprising in the neighboring French colony of Martinique, which was put down by the colonists. Saint-Domingue was soon to follow. What ensued was two years of chaos, during which all the interested actors tried to push their agendas. The colonists in Saint-Domingue realized that despite the collapse of the old order in France, the National Assembly was not exactly their ally. They armed themselves and decided to act independently, even organizing the Colonial Assembly and drawing up their own constitution by May 1790.

Meanwhile, the free people of color believed that the revolution would finally change their lives. Their representatives in France allied with the local Society of the Friends of the Blacks, an abolitionist group that had been founded in Paris in February 1788. Julien Raimond, a free man of color from Saint-Domingue who had inherited a plantation with over 100 slaves from his white colonist father, had traveled to France in 1785 to lobby the French government for equal rights for other free people of color in the colonies. Along with others, he tried to accelerate the adoption of laws that would look at free people of color as equals to the white colonists.

Vincent Ogé, a Creole-turned-revolutionary, sailed back to Saint-Domingue from Paris in October 1790 and led an armed revolt in the northern part of the colony. Ogé had been a rich mixed-race individual from Saint-Domingue who owned substantial property in Le Cap. Despite surprising the white colonists with his revolt, he was quickly overpowered and forced to flee to Spanish Santo Domingo, where Spanish officials captured and surrendered him to the colonists in Saint-Domingue. Ogé and his followers were trialed, arrested, and executed in the spring of 1791.

When the news of Ogé's revolt reached Paris, the National Assembly was forced to more seriously consider the fate of the people of color in the colonies. The antagonism that had always existed between the white colonists and the free people of color in Saint-Domingue had materialized into an armed insurrection. This meant it could inspire other similar rebellions. If the issue was not promptly dealt with, the turmoil in Saint-Domingue would have adverse economic effects on France itself. Thus, in May 1791, the National Assembly voted for a law proposed by the deputy Jean-François Rewbell. The law, which would eventually pass with a clear majority, granted free people of color whose parents had also been free full political rights in the colonies. Though the law only affected a minority of the free black population of Saint-Domingue, it was revered as a major victory for abolitionists, not only in Paris but also in London and the US—the other centers of such movements at the time.

For the colonists in Saint-Domingue, the "Rewbell Amendment," as the new act came to be known, complicated matters even more. The question of equality aside, the amendment set an important precedent of the National Assembly making a big decision regarding colonial affairs. The assembly had also decided to appoint a three-member civil commission that would travel to Saint-Domingue to oversee the law's implementation and directly report back to Paris. The colonists believed this further violated their rights of self-governance. The colonists and their Parisian representatives thus launched a vicious counter-campaign that convinced the National Assembly to overturn the decision in September 1791. However, as the protectors of white colonial rights were celebrating their victory in France, they were unaware that something massive had happened in Saint-Domingue in August 1791, the news of which had not yet reached Europe. It was the slave revolt that would kickstart the Haitian Revolution.

Chapter Two – Igniting the Spark

In this chapter, we will explore the origins of the 1791 uprisings that caught the French colonists off-guard and eventually grew into a full-blown revolution a few years later. Many figures that would come to shape the future Haitian Republic began their rise to prominence as participants in these movements, which the colonists at first regarded as simple rebellions. And, while there were two movements that began around the same time in Saint-Domingue, it is important to recognize that they were completely independent of each other. In later chapters, we will see how these initial distinctions between the two would affect Haitian society many years later.

Two Uprisings

The exact origins of the slave uprising that began in northern Saint-Domingue in August 1791 are unclear. Most accounts of the rebellion historians have assembled to reconstruct the events of the insurrection that would turn into the full revolution were written by white colonists. What is known is that a group of slaves assembled on August 14, eight days before the rebellion began, on a large plantation close to Le Cap. Among them were the slave *commandeurs*, who were in positions that allowed them to communicate with each other from one plantation to another. There, they drew up plans for a large-scale insurrection that involved launching simultaneous attacks on their respective masters and plantations.

Two days later, on August 16, a group of slaves acted too soon, trying to set fire to buildings on their plantations, which was not part of the original plan. The conspiracy was not revealed. A week after their initial meeting, on August 21, slaves met again at a place now known as Bois Caïman, seemingly to perform vodou ceremonies—something that would seem normal to the white masters. At the meeting, they decided to quickly proceed with their plans, believing that the white slaveowners might have felt that a larger attack was coming after the incident on the sixteenth. The slaves, with their leader Dutty Boukman, decided to act the next day.

Cooperating precisely and to the dismay of the colonists, the slaves began viciously attacking their respective plantations on August 22, 1791. They set fire to the precious sugar cane fields of the northern province at night, acting quickly and decisively, and stormed the lavish houses of the plantation owners. Planters fled to the towns, which they thought were better defended, abandoning their possessions. The insurrection was like an avalanche—it kept gaining momentum as hours went by, with more and more slaves rising up against their masters and contributing to the rebellion with whatever means they could.

Fear spread quickly among the white planters, who had never suspected that slaves would have been able to concentrate their forces together for a common goal. Compared to the insurrectionists, the white planters were very disorganized and paranoid, suspecting that every black man and woman around them was part of the conspiracy. Afraid, those whose plantations had survived the initial days of the revolt began capturing and shooting the slaves at their estates.

In Le Cap, the free people of color were also persecuted, suspected of supporting the uprising. Some believed free people of color had agitated the slaves to rise up, while others sought their help to fight against the slaves. Everything was at stake for the colonists, who now believed they had enemies everywhere. Governor-General Blanchelande appealed for help from neighboring colonies, thinking that without military support the slaves might break through the defenses and taken Le Cap. Meanwhile, the insurrection continued to gain momentum for about two months. By October 1791, the slaves had essentially driven the white colonists out of the eastern part of the northern province.

The fears of the colonists were confirmed when, at the same time as the slave uprising was gaining pace, the free people of color also revolted in the southern and western provinces of Saint-Domingue. The colonists now thought that a general anti-white conspiracy existed and that the two groups had acted in tandem. In reality, however, the free people of color rose up wanting political equality with the white colonists, outraged that they did not want to enforce the Rewbell Amendment laws adopted in May. A crucial aspect of their rebellion was that the abolition of slavery was not in their immediate demands. In fact, many free people of color recruited and paid black slaves from the rural plantations of western and southern provinces to fight for them. Their revolt was inspired more by the ongoing spirit of the French Revolution and the principles of individual liberty it propagated. Many individuals who played a key role in the later stages of the Haitian Revolution began their revolutionary activities as part of this rebellion as free people of color, including future presidents of the Republic of Haiti—Alexandre Pétion and Jean-Pierre Boyer.

Initial Setbacks

Despite catching the white colonists off guard, it became clear after October that the slave uprising could not continue at the same pace as it had begun in late August. There were an array of problems the slaves had to face, problems any revolutionary movement that aims to gain mass support faces at one point or another.

First of all, the movement lacked a clear objective. Slaves knew they were fighting for their freedom, but how exactly that freedom was to be achieved was still a big question. Killing their white masters en masse and burning their possessions was a possible answer, for sure, and an answer that may have been endorsed by the majority—but what next?

In addition, slaves were ill-equipped, leading them to rely more on numbers to overwhelm the white colonists, who managed to consolidate their forces weeks after the beginning of the rebellion. The colonists estimated that about a fifth of the slaves were armed with guns, while the majority would either rush their enemies with bare hands or use farming tools as weapons. Added to this were the communication problems among the rebels. It became increasingly difficult to organize precise attacks as their numbers grew.

All in all, by the end of the year, the colonists had suffered about 400 or so casualties, while an estimated 4,000 or more slaves had been killed and many captured.

General Philibert François Rouxel de Blanchelande played a leading role in organizing the defense of the white colonists. He established a line of forts in the narrow mountainous passes that connected the northern and western provinces to dissuade the slaves from potentially crossing and reaching Port-au-Prince or joining their forces with the free people of color. The initial leader of the rebellion, Dutty Boukman, was killed in a clash with the white colonists in early November, something they saw as a great victory they hoped would demoralize the slaves.

As for the free people of color, they were disappointed to learn of the decision of the National Assembly to void the Rewbell Amendment in September. Paris had agreed to leave the fate of the free people of color in the hands of the colonists in Saint-Domingue, another victory for the colonists. Before learning of this decision, the free people of color had believed that they had fought for the rights given to them by the National Assembly in May. Now, their movement did not seem as legitimate.

The news of the repealing of the Rewbell Amendment was brought to the colony by the first three-person civil commission from Paris, which instantly began motions to stabilize matters in the colony. They communicated their desires with the newly emerged leaders of the slave uprising—Jean-François and Georges Biassou—who had reorganized the efforts of the slaves after a brief halt in their advances since late October. The commissioners, whose main interest was to return things to the status quo for the colonial profits to flow back to France, were ready to pardon the slaves in exchange for them returning to work on the plantations. Biassou and Jean-François, on the other hand, wished to at least gain political freedoms and rights for themselves and other leaders of the revolt and were ready to persuade other slaves to end the fighting and return to work. This is a theme that would repeat many times throughout the course of the Haitian Revolution. There would be many instances when a number of leaders of the uprising would try to negotiate for their personal gain, ignoring the wants of the larger masses of black people, whether freemen or slaves.

All in all, the negotiations fell through. The colonists rejected the counterproposal of the black leaders, knowing they would receive the reinforcement of 6,000 men from France early the following year. A stalemate thus developed in the northern province.

Meanwhile, the free people of color were making steady advances in the southern and western provinces of Saint-Domingue. They had surrounded Port-au-Prince and had overcome much of the resistance from the colonists by the time the negotiations were taking place in Le Cap. A pivotal part of their success was the formation of an armed slave squadron that besieged the capital and forced a surrender from the colonists inside Port-au-Prince. The name of this group was "the Swiss," a nod to the professional Swiss soldiers that fought as mercenaries in French and other European armies.

However, the negotiations between the leaders of the free people of color and the white colonists would also take a dark turn. The colonists, who agreed to accept the political demands of the free people of color, also demanded a disbandment of "the Swiss" and the expulsion of its members from the colony. The free people of color agreed, disarming the squadron and shipping its members off to Jamaica to be resold into slavery. Many slave mercenaries managed to escape their re-enslavement but were murdered by white people, who distrusted them for betraying their masters.

This incident would later fuel the constant disagreements between the free people of color and the enslaved black population of Saint-Domingue over the course of the revolution. The fate of "the Swiss" was especially tragic, as it did not achieve a lasting peace between the colonists and the free people of color. Antagonism did not cease between the two groups, and many independent formations began emerging throughout the rural areas of the southern and western provinces, including separate slave uprisings. By 1792, thus, the cohesion of the movement of the free people of color had essentially been destroyed. The southern and western provinces of Saint-Domingue were in far more chaos than the north, where a stalemate had emerged between the colonists and the slaves.

Chaos in Saint-Domingue

In October 1791, the National Assembly was reorganized into the Legislative Assembly, and some figures with interests in the matters unfolding in Saint-Domingue managed to cement themselves into leading positions. One such individual, Jacques-Pierre Brissot, a leading activist in the Society of the Friends of the Blacks, thus pushed the question of racial segregation back into the national revolutionary agenda. Brissot favored re-granting free people of color equal political rights as white people in the colonies, believing that normalizing relations between these two groups would lead to the end of the slave rebellion.

Brissot and his lobby, who were careful not to suggest the abolition of slavery to other lawmakers because they were aware of the negative economic effects it would have on France, reached their goals in the spring of 1792. In early April, the king signed a law that granted full political and civil rights to free people of color in the colonies and dispatched an additional reinforcing army of 6,000 men to Saint-Domingue. To ensure the new decision would be properly upheld this time, the Legislative Assembly also sent a new civil commission, led by Étienne Polverel and Léger-Félicité Sonthonax. Both were members of the radical Jacobin club that had publicly opposed slavery.

Before the reinforcements and the new civil commission got to Saint-Domingue, however, the leaders of the slave uprising managed to thoroughly reorganize. After the failed negotiations, Jean-François and Biassou established a large network of fortified camps, each with a designated commander. One such commander was Toussaint Louverture, who had played an important role as a facilitator between the leaders of the slave rebels and the white colonists during the previous negotiations. Louverture had been a freed Creole when the revolt broke out in August of 1791, working for his former master Bayon de Libertat, with whom he had developed a close relationship. During the negotiations, he had urged the leaders of the slave uprising to push for more moderate demands and did not wish to jeopardize the talks, being in favor of a solution that would be acceptable to both parties. Over the next few months, he would demonstrate the skills and political craftsmanship that would eventually lead him to become the main figure in the revolution.

Despite reorganization, however, the goals of the slave uprising were still ill-defined in early 1792. The movement was not as united as one might believe. Jean-François and Biassou, with most other leaders of the newly established camp system, were almost considered an elite class themselves. They implemented regular working tribunals and councils in the territories they controlled. From the onset, they began creating a new society with military leaders at the top of the hierarchy, which seemed natural to most of the former slaves. The lands taken from the white colonists were redistributed among them, providing the basis for a new post-revolutionary peasant class. Interestingly, Biassou and other leaders urged the ordinary black people to go back to working these lands almost immediately when there was a stalemate in the conflict. Most saw themselves as potentially the replacers of the old rich white colonists. They would own most of the plantations, and the slaves would work for them. This became especially clear once the leaders of the slave uprising began selling other slaves, mostly those unfit to fight, to the neighboring

Spanish Santo Domingo for supplies such as weapons and clothes.

Many black people had never lived outside of the slavery system and thus imagined a post-revolutionary society where the practice would be continued but modified, no longer containing its most violent elements. The concepts of individual rights and freedoms, which were the driving forces behind the contemporary revolutionary movement in France, had not fully penetrated the minds of the slaves, including their leaders.

In essence, the revolutionaries in Paris had not progressed to outlawing slavery and were even radically against religion. This was offensive to the black people in Saint-Domingue, as Catholicism played a big part in their lives. Jean-François and Biassou thus expressed their support for the king, not the revolutionaries, reacting strongly to the news of Louis XVI's imprisonment. If anything, it was the white colonists and not the former slaves who were pro-revolution despite having a dubious relationship with the National Assembly.

By the time the Second Civil Commission arrived in Saint-Domingue in September 1792, the situation had become even more chaotic. The new civil commissioners were determined to carry out the law adopted in April that granted equal political and civil rights to the free people of color, which would transform Saint-Domingue into one of the most egalitarian New World societies.

General Blanchelande, who had proceeded to suffer heavy defeats against the insurrectionists in the southern province, was sent back to France by the new civil commission. His defeats were used in the new Revolutionary Tribunal in April 1793 as evidence of his counter-revolutionary activities, leading to him being condemned to death by the guillotine. The new civil commissioners, upon their arrival, publicly stated that it was not their intention to abolish slavery, winning support from the colonists. This declaration was necessary, as the radical Jacobin revolutionaries had proclaimed that the principles of liberty, equality, and fraternity should be applied to everyone living in French territories, a statement that had been received warily by the colonists. Still, as many colonists would rather see the free people of color as their equals than as slaves, they cooperated with the civil commissioners who set up a new body of governance with an equal number of black and white leaders.

Commissioners Sonthonax and Polverel did face some resistance, mostly from the *petit blancs* who had more reasons to oppose the granting of freedoms to mixed-race people. However, they established firm relations with the free men of color, granting them the opportunity to form armed militias, which they used to overpower the *petit blanc* groups that called for white supremacy in Saint-Domingue. From early 1793, in fact, white colonial militiamen, the freshly arrived troops from France, and the armed free people of color launched collective offensives against the slave insurgents in the northern and southern provinces. This alliance was made possible by not only the direct efforts of Sonthonax and Polverel in enforcing the new egalitarian laws but also the slave leaders' royalist sympathies.

They saw great success. The fortified positions of slave insurgents in the northern province were almost fully taken, with thousands of them falling as prisoners. Biassou and Jean-François were forced to flee east toward the mountains, close to the Spanish border. The rich planters who had fled to the cities when the insurrection had begun became hopeful that they would soon be able to return to their plantations.

Painting of Commissioner Sonthonax, unknown painter.
https://commons.wikimedia.org/wiki/File:Sonthonax.jpg

However, almost as soon as the civil commissioners had managed to reestablish control over the colony, matters became even more complicated. On January 21, 1793, the revolutionaries in France guillotined King Louis XVI, an event that united Europe's major monarchies to join the war effort against France. Revolutionary France had been at war with Austria since the previous year, a conflict that had aimed to restore the image of the king, which had now been executed by the radical revolutionaries, led by Maximilien Robespierre. Both of France's main colonial rivals, Spain and Great Britain, thus declared war on France, hoping to end the dangers the revolution posed to the institution of the monarchy in Europe and benefit from the spoils of war, especially in the colonies.

In Saint-Domingue, this meant commissioners Sonthonax and Polverel, passionate Jacobin revolutionaries who followed orders from Paris, had to prepare for new threats.

What complicated things was that the British and the Spanish intended to exploit the chaotic situation in Saint-Domingue. In London, the representatives of the white colonists had met with the British government, declaring their support to a planned British invasion of Saint-Domingue in exchange for guaranteeing the continuance of slavery.

The Spanish, on the other hand, negotiated with the slave insurgents, promising them freedom if they fought for the Spanish armies against French Saint-Domingue. The Spanish and the slaves of Saint-Domingue had more in common than it might seem at first glance. The newly executed King Louis XVI, towards whom the slave leaders were sympathetic, was a member of the Bourbon royal family that also ruled Spain. The Spanish were devout Catholics firmly against the French revolutionaries who had disrespected the religion, much like the slaves.

First Emancipation Proclamation

To deal with the Spanish and the British threats, the commissioners resorted to the previously successful method of forging better alliances with the free people of color. They ensured that the big cities were firmly under their control, trying to divert much of the fighting to the countryside. In May, with the arrival of the new governor, General François-Thomas Galbaud, they were forced to reexamine their strategies. Galbaud, a decorated veteran from France's European wars, did not share the commissioners' radical Jacobin ideas. In fact, he owned plantations with slaves in the colony. Sonthonax and Polverel deemed this dangerous to their efforts at reducing at least the observable inequality in the colony's society.

The commissioners set out to Cap-Français to meet the new governor and discuss their plans. But on June 20, General Galbaud, with the support of local agitated white colonists, stormed the city's streets. Though the attack was repelled mostly by the squads of free men of color who sympathized with the commissioners, Sonthonax and Polverel were forced to flee the city to the nearby village of Haut du Cap. Before they left, however, they spread the promise of freedom to any black slave who would agree to fight with them against Galbaud.

By the next day, thousands of slaves had appeared, ready to join Sonthonax and Polverel's side in exchange for freedom. They were all sworn into the army and armed as much as the situation allowed. On June 21, the commissioners led these reinforcements into Le Cap, where brutal fighting ensued for the next few days. The city's population was fearful and in disarray, confused about who was fighting on whose side. Many buildings were burned, and hundreds, including Galbaud and his men, had to flee on ships.

By the 23rd, the commissioners, who were now in charge of a much larger army, found themselves victorious, but at a great cost. Disorganized fighting and urban violence had led to one of the most tragic episodes of the revolution as of then, with over 3,000 civilian and military casualties. Cap-Français, one of the most prosperous cities of the New World, largely lay in ruins.

Despite this, the battle marked a turning point for the ongoing situation in Saint-Domingue. Granting freedom to slaves who fought for the commissioners marked a significant precedent. Soon, however, they realized that they still did not have the support of most of the black population. Most experienced contingents of the slave uprising, including those commanded by Biassou, Jean-François, and Louverture, remained firmly on the Spanish side despite efforts to convince them to join the commissioners. In fact, in the letters of that summer, Louverture reasserted his loyalty to the Bourbon monarchy and rejected the offer to switch sides.

Thus, in August 1793, Sonthonax and Polverel took the most radical decision of the Haitian Revolution, proclaiming a general emancipation of slaves in Saint-Domingue. Every former slave, women included, was now a free French citizen with full rights and the principles of the Declaration of the Rights of Man and Citizen applying to them. The commissioners knew that this step would be controversial, at the very least. Neither was fully in favor of the abolition of slavery because they knew the economic importance of the colonies that were dependent on the institution. It was the urgency to gain military support that pushed them, hoping the slaves all over the colony would realize that fighting for revolutionary France (which the commissioners still represented) was the best choice they had. Neither Britain nor Spain had dared to declare general emancipation by that point, and the commissioners were banking on this.

To ensure emancipation would not spell the complete economic collapse of the colony if the war ended soon, the commissioners were careful to include a set of regulations and restrictions that essentially required the freed slaves to at first work on their respective plantations. However, they were also ready to profoundly change their attitude toward former slave labor, for example, proposing changes in the language defining former slaves. Thus, the former slaves were referred to as *cultivateurs*, while the former *commandeurs* were called *conducteurs*. The *cultivateurs*, according to the new system, would earn a share of the profit from the plantations they resided on but were still required to largely fulfill their previous duties. It's clear that the nature of this modification was heavily inspired by the French Revolution, which had also renamed many old aspects of French society, including institutions and even the months of the calendar. In addition to pay, the freed slaves got better general working conditions and rest days, and the previously legal punishments against former slaves were declared void.

All in all, the first emancipation declaration issued by commissioners Sonthonax and Polverel in August 1793 was a massive step towards the future, contributing to building a slave-free society in the French colony of Saint-Domingue. The decision yielded modest results initially, with fewer slaves switching sides to join the colonial army against France's enemies. Still, it clearly spelled out that French Saint-Domingue, not Spain or Britain, was where slaves would at least technically be considered fully equal to white settlers. Though it was still early to discuss the implementation of such measures, the safety of Saint-Domingue, or even of the existence of a national fervor that would lead to the transformation of the colony into Haiti, the proclamation proved to be a crucial breaking point.

Chapter Three – The Flames of Freedom

In this chapter, we will see how the situation in Saint-Domingue unfolded after the dramatic decision by the Second Civil Commission to issue partial emancipation in the colony. The next few months would turn out to be critical for the fate of the Haitian Revolution. The central government in Paris would proceed to officially abolish slavery as a legal institution in the colony in 1794. This decision, which stemmed from the revolutionary spirits that were as high as ever in France at the time, would drastically shape the outcome of the Haitian Revolution. We will also look at the origins of a former black slave and general of the black uprising who would eventually play an immense in the history of Haiti– Toussaint Louverture.

Abolition

The proclamation of the emancipation of slaves in Saint-Domingue by civil commissioners Sonthonax and Polverel had been a major step toward swinging the tides of the ongoing conflict in favor of revolutionary France. It had certainly created an incentive for many black people who were fighting with the British and the Spanish to consider switching sides.

Additionally, by mid-1793, news from Europe highlighted the fact that France was doing quite well in the war against the coalition, which included every major power of the continent. This provided another reason for the black people in Saint-Domingue to enlist in the French colonial forces.

Spanish officials in Santo Domingo resorted to dubious tactics, trying to secretly gain support from the French white colonists by guaranteeing the return of their properties after the end of the war. This promise directly conflicted with the one they had made to the fighters of the slave uprising, further complicating the matter. Nevertheless, most black leaders, Biassou and Jean-François included, were still on the Spanish side. Still, as their interests came increasingly in conflict with one another, anything was prone to happen in the colonial war.

The National Convention in France and the radical Committee of Public Safety that had been created to "ensure security during the time of crisis," on the other hand, decided to recall the civil commissioners for abusing their powers in July 1793. The news reached Saint-Domingue in September, a month after the commissioners had proceeded with their emancipation. What followed was a decision issued by the National Convention that fully turned the tide of the situation in Saint-Domingue. On 16 Pluviôse Year II according to the French Revolutionary Calendar (February 4, 1794), the National Convention officially abolished the institution of slavery in all of France's colonies, granting citizenship to all men of the colonies, with full rights guaranteed by the constitution.

The decree, which passed with narrow support in the National Convention, had only recently found itself on the busy agenda of the revolutionaries, who were more concerned with the ongoing war than the question of slavery. It emerged as a prominent issue thanks to the extensive work of a three-person lobby sent from Saint-Domingue to France by Commissioner Sonthonax in June 1793. The group consisted of white colonist Louis Dufay, Jean-Baptiste Mills (a free man of color), and a free black army officer named Jean-Baptiste Belley, who had only reached Paris in January 1794.

As representatives of the north province of Saint-Domingue, they sought the convention's endorsement of the emancipation proclamation. Their main argument was perhaps what the members of the National Convention wanted to hear—that the emancipated blacks would eagerly fight on the side of the French against their colonial enemies, providing a huge numerical superiority. The lobby tried to make it clear that the emancipation proposed by Sonthonax and Polverel included restrictions so their proposition would seem less radical. However, perhaps partially to celebrate universal human rights and cement the importance of their decision in history, the National Convention decided to go further than proposed and grant full freedoms and rights to all free men of color in the colonies.

The news of this historic decree reached Saint-Domingue in June 1794. The reaction was mixed, as many of the white colonists in Saint-Domingue were outraged, uncertain of their economic future. Commissioners Sonthonax and Polverel, who had somehow maintained control of the colony for revolutionary France during the most turbulent of times, were (as mentioned) ordered to leave the colony for their case to be investigated by the National Convention. The governorship of Saint-Domingue was entrusted to General Laveaux, commander of the French colonial forces under the commissioners.

Still, the situation in the colony was far from resolved. In the same month, the British forces that had occupied some territories in the southern and western provinces reached Port-au-Prince (renamed Port-Républicain) and captured it. More importantly, despite the abolition of slavery and the granting of full rights to men of color in the French colonies, it was still a long time before the decree was fully implemented. And no one really knew why. The society of Saint-Domingue was not ready for such a profound transformation.

It all became more complicated when Maximilien Robespierre's radical "Reign of Terror" in Paris was overthrown the next month, on July 27, 1974, in what became known as the Thermidorian Reaction. Robespierre, the main leader of the radical republicans, was put to the guillotine, and the Thermidorians began to reform France into a more moderate republic. This included the disbandment of many radical institutions and a general decentralization of power throughout the country. Importantly, it also included reversing most of the policies taken during the Reign of Terror from 1793 to 1794. The white colonists' lobby in Paris campaigned extensively for the annulment of the abolition of slavery, a decree they considered a product of the crazy radicalism of Robespierre's regime. The fate of the conflict in Saint-Domingue now rested on the decision of the more moderate members of the National Convention. However, a decisive development that would change the course of the war had already happened in Saint-Domingue in May 1794. A month before the original news of the abolition decree had reached the colony, Toussaint Louverture had switched his allegiance from the Spanish to the French.

Toussaint Louverture

Just like many other aspects of his early career as a prominent figure of the Haitian Revolution, the reasons behind Louverture joining the French forces remain unclear. The most probable cause was his ongoing conflict with other black leaders who also fought for the Spanish in early 1794. He declared his allegiance to the French in May, shortly before the news of the abolition decree reached Cap-Français, and it is unlikely he heard about it before June.

Nevertheless, when he appeared before the soon-to-be-made governor, General Laveaux, with his force of about 4,000 former slaves, he asked for forgiveness, declaring his support for revolutionary ideals. Louverture also claimed that he had been deceived by the Spanish, who, according to him, were also manipulating other black fighters. His decision to come to the French side was welcomed by commissioners Sonthonax and Polverel before they were taken to Paris that summer to be investigated by the National Convention. They saw it as an obvious advantage for their cause. Toussaint and his men controlled a large stretch of forts in the mountains that connected northern and western provinces, cutting off the Spanish possessions in the east and the British-occupied lands on the western coast.

Toussaint Louverture by Alexandre-François-Louis, Comte de Girardin.
https://commons.wikimedia.org/wiki/File:Toussaint_Louverture_-_Girardin.jpg

Toussaint possessed an intriguing persona from the beginning, as we mentioned above. As a freed former slave before the outbreak of the uprising in 1791, he was unlike the thousands of black slaves he would come to lead in the next few years. He had been freed about fifteen years before the uprising and, during that time, had significantly grown his possessions, which included a modest farm with a few slaves. By the time of the rebellion, he had sold his property to live with and work for his former master. His wife and children were still slaves at the time.

Toussaint knew how to read and write and was quite well-spoken in French. To achieve a higher level of literacy, he hired white secretaries to teach him throughout the early stages of the uprising. He also made efforts to better inform himself about the ongoing situation in Europe, realizing that the conflict in Saint-Domingue was closely tied to European affairs.

This, combined with his political craftsmanship, contributed to his quick rise as at least the third most prominent leader of the slave uprising behind Jean-François and Biassou. Though he did not have much military experience, he was not ashamed to admit it and heavily relied on the advice of more experienced officers, both white and black, throughout the years.

All of this can be inferred from his regular correspondence with General Laveaux, where he appears as a wise and careful leader who built on the lessons of past actions to proceed successfully with new decisions. From the beginning of the chaos in Saint-Domingue, Toussaint Louverture acted with great diligence.

Though his political leanings are unknown, he quickly adapted to every situation he was put into, realizing that the war in the colony could only end with a complete societal change in which black people were better integrated with the white population. His good relations with the different interested groups thus awarded him leeway to side with each based on whoever was in a better place at the time. For example, when he decided to finally side with the French forces in 1794, he was quick to publicly embrace those principles upon which the French Revolution had progressed for years. He asserted his belief in universal equality and the abolition of slavery.

However, Toussaint was more careful to properly spell out his objectives than former slaves who wished to fully take over the lands of the white colonists for themselves, for example. He knew that such radical steps could not be successfully taken at once and was in favor of transforming the colonial society little by little, something that would eventually pit him against many of the rural *cultivateurs.*

Despite his support for the republican cause, he also showed a lot of individualism. Paired with his political skills, this earned him a great reputation even in continental France, where republican newspapers proudly mentioned him as a leader of French Saint-Domingue as early as 1795. His identification with French revolutionary ideals did not spell his abandonment of the Catholic religion, as it had in France since 1789. His religiosity was one of the reasons he was seen as an inspiring commander by most of the black people who chose to follow him.

All these reasons contributed to Toussaint's rapid rise to prominence as a leader of the slave movement in northern Saint-Domingue. It was as if he had an aura around him that had destined him to become the most crucial part of the uprising.

This is not to say no other leaders were emerging at the same time. In the south, Commissioner Polverel had made military commander André Rigaud the governor of the southern province when he left for Paris in the summer of 1794. Rigaud had distinguished himself as an early commander of the free people of color and had contributed greatly to keeping the British in check in that part of Saint-Domingue. As a free man of color, however, his personality and goals were rather different from those of Louverture, leading to the two eventually emerging as rivals, though they both fought for France.

Rigaud had declared his support for the revolutionary cause much earlier than Toussaint and, in the eyes of Commissioner Polverel, had earned his position as governor of the south. The regiment he commanded was mostly made up of black slaves, but men of color served as officers. This was typical behavior from someone who considered himself above the black slaves as a former wealthy and elite free person of color.

Another circumstance contributed to Toussaint's rise to prominence as a revered black leader. In July of 1795, Spain lost the war against France in Europe and, according to the terms of the Peace of Basel, was forced to cede control of Santo Domingo to the French. This meant France was now fully in control of the island of Hispaniola and that French Saint-Domingue had more than doubled in size. It also meant that Spanish armies would have to leave the island, and they promptly did. Many of the black slave leaders went with them, including Biassou and Jean-François.

However, the majority of the black fighters who had sided with the Spanish decided to join their forces with Toussaint—a man they knew could lead them successfully. Toussaint was now the only prominent leader from the original slave uprising, disregarding whether he had played any part in starting the uprising (at least those at the time fully believed he had). Toussaint gladly accepted thousands of blacks to his side, now as free citizens of France. He was thus promoted to the rank of a general of French armies by Governor-General Laveaux, which would later be approved by the National Convention in Paris.

Toussaint used the reinforcements to deal with an unexpected attempted coup by a commander named Jean-Baptiste (Jean-Louis) Villatte in March 1796, a free man of color. Villatte's coup was seen as a direct challenge to the French colonial authority by Governor-General Laveaux, who was taken captive by the insurgents as they stormed the cities of Cap-Français. White citizens in Saint-Domingue and France had most feared that a non-white man, let alone one that was not centrally appointed, would take control of the colony.

Toussaint marched to Le Cap from his base in the mountainous region of the western province after several former black officers of Villatte's army appealed to him. The coup was deemed an attempt to assert the dominance of free colored people in Saint-Domingue and was directly defeated by Toussaint—a black former slave who now commanded the forces of revolutionary France. Toussaint freed Laveaux, who once again promoted him, this time to the rank of deputy governor of the northern province.

This incident once again increased the influence of Toussaint in Saint-Domingue, and he gained control of even more forces that had previously served under Villatte. The defeat was saluted by the French, who saw Toussaint's actions as those of a loyal general serving his country. Interestingly, Toussaint would also later used the attempted coup as his argument against the free people of color of Saint-Domingue, whose selfish acts had seen grave consequences.

The Third Civil Commission

In the summer of 1795, the National Convention adopted a new constitution for France, creating an institution known as the Directory, a committee of five members who would jointly govern the country for the foreseeable future. The Directory, though created as a more moderate institution in a more moderate France, decided not to go back on the decision of the still-radical National Convention to abolish slavery a year earlier.

In addition, in the fall of 1795, the investigation of the possible abuse of power by the Second Civil Commission of Saint-Domingue, (Sonthonax and Polverel) was concluded. The investigation found both commissioners innocent, though Commissioner Polverel had passed away due to illness before the verdict was announced. In January of the following year, the French government decided to send the Third Civil Commission to the colony, mainly to oversee the integration of the Spanish portion of Hispaniola. Commissioner Sonthonax would return in a leading role, now with the status of the man who had greatly contributed to the general emancipation. With him were the new members of the commission: Julien Raimond, a veteran activist and free man of color, Philippe Roume, a former member of the First Civil Commission who was tasked with dealing with the former Spanish territories, and two other officials—Marc Antoine Giraud and Pierre Leblanc. The Third Civil Commission was also accompanied by 1,200 reinforcements and military supplies to properly arm the black soldiers, who had been fighting undersupplied since 1791.

The new commission set sail in April 1796, arriving in Cap-Français just after the conclusion of the unsuccessful coup d'état. Its arrival created new power dynamics, at first between the commissioners and free people of color in the southern part of the colony. As you may remember, General Rigaud, the commander of these regiments, had cemented himself as a reputable figure in southern Saint-Domingue, where he had held off the British advance in hopes of reinforcements. When his authority was challenged by the commissioners, who sent their representatives to take control of the initiative, Rigaud and his men were outraged over what they saw as a clear provocation. They caused disturbances in the city of Cayes in August 1796, targeting the white population in the city, perhaps as a sign of revenge against the commissioners. Sonthonax and his company failed to establish firm control over the southern province, while Rigaud, who held distinct views about the future of the colony, gained more influence.

The commission failed to establish good relations with Toussaint Louverture, as well. By the time of the commission's arrival, Louverture had become a revered leader of the uprising in Saint-Domingue and beyond. Commissioner Sonthonax and Louverture had had a complicated relationship before the former departed for Paris in 1794, starting as rivals fighting for opposite camps but eventually coming together after Toussaint decided to switch sides in the spring of 1794. Back then, Sonthonax, after being ordered to leave the colony, commended Toussaint for joining the right side, not the least because he had swung the tide of the conflict in French favor. However, Toussaint had accrued considerably more influence while Sonthonax was absent and was not exactly eager to cede authority to the commissioner after his arrival.

Two factors made the relationship between the two more complicated. Firstly, former slaves and free people of color liked Sonthonax for having led the emancipation movement, as well as for his efforts in the war against the Spanish and the British. Secondly, Toussaint continued to increase his standing after the arrival of Sonthonax by achieving considerable success against the British forces. In fact, it was partly because the British were unable to fully route Toussaint's forces that they would slowly reduce their commitment to occupying Saint-Domingue, with fewer and fewer reinforcements over 1796 and 1797.

By this point, Toussaint most likely already had an independent vision for the future of Saint-Domingue. He was not keen on the French re-establishing full control over the colony, a sign of which had been the arrival of the Third Civil Commission.

Instead of resorting to a coup against Sonthonax, however, which would make him a clear target of the French, he manipulated the circumstances in his favor. In August 1796, in the elections organized by the new commission to elect representatives for the colony in the affairs of the new French government, he declared his support for Commissioner Sonthonax and Governor-General Laveaux. Toussaint supported the idea that white leaders with experience were necessary to properly represent Saint-Domingue in the Directory's legislative assembly, and his numerous followers agreed. Commissioner and former lobbyist for emancipation in Paris, Julien Raimond, also sided with Toussaint.

Governor-General Laveaux was easily persuaded to leave for Paris, but Commissioner Sonthonax showed more reluctance. He recognized that Toussaint was essentially getting rid of him and tried to put up a last stand to challenge his authority in the colony. However, a few circumstances made his resistance feeble, to say the least. Firstly, with the eventual departure of Laveaux, Toussaint would become the commander of all colonial forces in Saint-Domingue, further increasing his power and influence. Secondly, in the elections of April 1797 in Paris, moderate and counterrevolutionary lawmakers won a considerable number of seats, calling for more direct French control over the colonies, with some even suggesting the reinstitution of slavery. The latter occurrence prompted Toussaint to be more direct with the commissioner. In August 1797, he forced Sonthonax to leave by proposing an ultimatum, asserting his will (thanks to his military power) and escorting the commissioner with his loyal officers to a ship bound for France.

The expulsion of Commissioner Sonthonax from Saint-Domingue elevated Toussaint to the role of the clear administrative head of the colony, something that had been a long way in coming for a general who had slowly worked his way up the ranks of military and civil office. The population of Saint-Domingue knew of his skills that had helped him accrue popularity over the years, and, for most of them, the leadership of Toussaint Louverture seemed natural. Of course, his background as a former slave and the (historically unverifiable) notion that he had been involved in the uprising from the beginning further served to elevate his image.

Toussaint thus worked to win the hearts of the deputies in Paris, who reconfirmed their commitment to the revolutionary ideals of equality and liberty by once again asserting that black men were French citizens with full rights. The French government still considered Saint-Domingue a vital part of France's great colonial empire and certainly had a vision of bringing production back up to antebellum levels once things died down.

Toussaint, who did not necessarily agree with all the revolutionary concepts expressed by the Directory, nevertheless kept up regular correspondence with the government. In his letters, he urged the government to recognize that it had been thanks to the efforts of the free people of color and former black slaves that Saint-Domingue was still under French control. He stated that thanks to the earlier decrees adopted by the government that abolished slavery and guaranteed equal rights to the blacks, Saint-Domingue was ready to essentially govern itself and would soon be able to return to its crucial economic role for the motherland. Though this was not the full truth, as many aspects of the colony's future were still up in the air in late 1797, Toussaint Louverture's leadership seemed promising, to say the least. People in France and the colony were compelled to find out what this next stage would bring for Saint-Domingue.

Chapter Four – Toussaint's Saint-Domingue

In the following chapter, we will look at the transformation of Toussaint Louverture from one of the black generals who had accrued many victories during the uprising to a true leader of the revolutionary movement with his own vision for the future of the colony. When Toussaint consolidated his power and emerged as a black governor-general of Saint-Domingue, the revolutionary spirit had not yet become nationalistic and there were no talks of a fully independent state from France. On the other hand, thanks to his political maneuvers and charismatic personality, Toussaint Louverture would earn infamy as the man who would eventually even be regarded by Napoleon as his rival. This chapter will tell the story of how Toussaint slowly increased his influence over Saint-Domingue and eliminated his opponents to become the first black dictator of the colony—a trend that would continue even as Haiti gained its independence.

The New Saint-Domingue

The situation in Saint-Domingue in 1798—seven years after the beginning of the slave uprising—had certainly stabilized, but an aura of uncertainty had rightfully befallen the colony. The old distinctions based on race alone were gone, but efforts were still being undertaken to completely restructure Saint-Domingue and restore the way of life that had been distorted for years. Changes to the social life of the colony were being steadily implemented, some with more success than others.

For example, after decades of struggling, it was finally legal for the black population of the island to marry and have families. Many former slaves thus began legalizing their relationships (many of which had begun even before the insurrection in 1791), granting them a truer sense of belonging to a civilized society. Many blacks, who had chosen to remain on the plantations, could now benefit from better working days, a salary that was comparable to those of French laborers, and a set of regulations that prohibited all the old punishment methods. They could also now legally buy property and run businesses, which meant that they could accrue private wealth.

The colony's cities, which had been ruined by constant warfare, were also beginning to be reconstructed. There were clear signs of progress when it came to rebuilding Cap-Français, for example, which had suffered from the devastating fire in 1793. We know from contemporary memoirs and letters that many people participated in construction works to restore the old European image of the city. Many of its streets and squares were renamed to reflect the merits of the French Revolution, as had been the case for many cities in France. Visitors, foreign merchants, and returning French colonists remarked on the bustling social and economic life of Le Cap, which, though it was not yet back to previous levels, was certainly on its way. Many black citizens opened shops, where they practiced skills they had picked up during slavery, and contributed to the new urban life of the colony.

Crucially, after a series of unsuccessful offensives since late 1796 that resulted in thousands of casualties from fighting and disease, the British abandoned their efforts and left Saint-Domingue in 1798. The withdrawal of the British forces meant that the conflict in Saint-Domingue was officially over, with Toussaint Louverture credited by the population as the man who had defeated the invaders in the name of revolutionary France.

All these factors laid the foundation for the development of the colony in the future, but there were many obvious problems and uncertainties still apparent in Saint-Domingue. The biggest problem facing the newly transformed society of Saint-Domingue was the colony's completely disrupted economy and the unresolved question of what exactly to do with thousands of acres of plantation fields. Though the emancipation of black slaves had meant the deprivation of the labor that worked their fields, the French colonial government had been reluctant to proceed with a total redistribution of the lands previously owned by white planters.

One of the biggest complications in this regard was not only the destruction of many plantations throughout the fighting but also French laws regarding activities in French lands throughout the revolution. For example, the laws stated that individuals who had fled France during the revolution were to be declared rebels unless they had been forced to leave their homes to seek refuge in other French lands or neutral countries. When many plantation-owning refugees returned to their properties as the situation stabilized, French officials welcomed the idea of them holding on to these lands instead of dividing them into smaller portions and giving them to the freed population who did not possess any properties of their own. Sometimes, in the absence of former plantation owners, government-appointed managers would take over, a system that eventually benefitted no one as these managers were not equipped to properly run such huge lands.

Thus, during the days of the civil commission, officials adopted a policy of giving the lands to wealthy individuals who had the means of running the estates without significant drops in production. In this way, many black and free generals and state officials of color— Toussaint, Rigaud, and Julien Raimond included—were granted sizeable lands of their own. This created clearer divides between the richer and poorer people of the original uprising. For example, poorer black people who had fewer resources to manage such estates (many of whom ran parts of the old plantations) emigrated to the less prosperous mountainous regions of the colony and lived their lives as subsistence farmers. This societal divide would form the basis of the peasant society that would eventually emerge in Haiti over the nineteenth century.

The uncertain nature of land ownership in post-insurrection Saint-Domingue made it very difficult to get agricultural production back to pre-insurrection levels. An additional contributing factor was the departure of the agricultural workforce, which had been made up of slaves, into other jobs and trades, now that the formerly enslaved population had become free.

A major aspect of this workforce migration was the increasingly militarized society of Saint-Domingue. After the withdrawal of the British, forces under Toussaint's command numbered 25,000, most of whom were former slaves who had worked the fields before 1791. This did not include the men under Rigaud's leadership in the southern part of the colony—a force comparable to Toussaint's. This meant that in 1798, at least 10 percent of the population was part of the army, contributing to Saint-Domingue's inability to keep up its agricultural output.

This, paired with undereducation, meant that profound, long-term changes to improve the quality of life of the colony's black population were not being taken. The colony, for example, had no secondary education system, even for its wealthier white population. Before 1791, richer families of Saint-Domingue sent their kids abroad to France to study, a practice that was encouraged by the French government, which had only after the revolution decided to build accessible public schools.

Toussaint Consolidates

As mentioned, after the departure of Commissioner Sonthonax in August 1797, Toussaint Louverture was now the most powerful man in Saint-Domingue. Other representatives of the French government remained in the colony (including Commissioner Roume, who was in the formerly Spanish Santo Domingo), but there was no doubt about Toussaint's authority.

General Rigaud still held considerable influence in Saint-Domingue, commanding a large force in the southern province, but Toussaint avoided direct confrontation with Rigaud. Rigaud, who had played a major role throughout the conflict, certainly did not regard Toussaint as his superior, and the southern province under him largely operated autonomously even as Toussaint accrued more power. Nevertheless, from late 1797 until the withdrawal of the British forces from Saint-Domingue, the two chose to cooperate, recognizing their main common enemy at the time.

General Thomas Maitland, the commander of the British forces in the colony, decided to slowly organize the withdrawal of his forces to minimize losses. Despite suffering defeats at the hands of the forces commanded by Rigaud and Toussaint respectively, Maitland tried to complicate the relationship between the two generals by clearly regarding Toussaint to be above Rigaud. This would eventually contribute to the pre-existing rivalry.

Meanwhile, Toussaint made his ambitions and independent spirit known to his superiors in the French government, earning him an infamous reputation. Interestingly, at the time he was making independent decisions to sometimes undermine the framework imposed upon him by Paris, he was very much like an up-and-coming general, Napoleon Bonaparte.

The Directory, soon to be overthrown by Napoleon, sent General Joseph d'Hédouville as its new representative in Saint-Domingue in the spring of 1798. Hédouville's objective was to undermine Toussaint's authority and remind the people of Saint-Domingue that they were still subjects of France and the rule of the French government. A part of this mission, for example, was to make sure that the old white plantation owners got their estates back and continued agricultural production on the same scale as before—a goal that was largely unpopular among the black population.

Hédouville was aware of the influence of the black general, but it soon became clear that he had underestimated Toussaint's skills. Toussaint, echoing his previous actions, did not directly oppose the new representative of the French government but expressed his concerns that Hédouville's arrival might contribute to disorder in the colony, which had finally been on its way to full recovery. Thus, when the black population in the countryside of Cap-Français violently rose against the white planters, Toussaint claimed that it was impossible to pacify the situation as long as Hédouville remained in the colony. The French representative had already become quite unpopular due to introducing a policy that required former slaves to work on their former plantations for a minimum of three years in exchange for pay. This incident only contributed to him being forced to leave Saint-Domingue in October 1798.

However, before Hédouville sailed for France, disappointed that he could not carry out the main goal of his mission, he expressed his support for General Rigaud in the south, a sentiment he claimed came from the French government. Rigaud was officially granted equal status to Toussaint, driving the rivalry between the two even deeper.

Nevertheless, Hédouville's departure was a complete victory for Toussaint, who had by then proven to Paris that he was difficult to control. To create a sense that he still respected the central government, however, Toussaint called on the final white member of the Third Civil Commission, Commissioner Roume, to Cap-Français to replace Hédouville. Roume obviously lacked the power and sway to properly oppose Toussaint—exactly the reason he had been chosen by the black general in the first place.

Toussaint further asserted his position by demonstrating that he could act independently of what was, on paper, required of him from the French government. For example, he allowed white colonists who had sided with the British in hopes of increasing their autonomy from the French government to return to their properties. Paris had been against this since the beginning of the war, and Toussaint's decision thus directly conflicted with the will of the Directory.

In another otherwise unexpected move, Toussaint negotiated the reopening of trade with the United States, even as official relations between Paris and Washington had been shaky since 1793. The US and France had been engaged in a conflict known as the Quasi-War, which had started when Washington stopped repaying France for its help in the War of Independence. As a response to this and to distort trade between the US and Britain—France's main rival— the French government had allowed privateers to attack US merchant ships in 1796.

Toussaint thus sent his representative to Washington, assuring Congress that American ships would be safe in Saint-Domingue's ports. The Americans could not say no to reestablishing trade with Saint-Domingue, remembering that the colony produced goods that were universally consumed by its thriving communities. Despite opposition from Southern slaveowners, Congress passed an amendment that allowed US ships to enter Saint-Domingue's ports based on a mutual understanding with Toussaint. Soon, the black general would also allow British merchants to come and trade in Cap-Français. Toussaint and his inner circle of black officers, who had been enriched by their acquisition of plantations, immensely profited from these measures.

By 1799, Toussaint Louverture commanded a large army and the most prosperous of the colony's lands. He was revered for his personality and political skill and was rightfully considered a vital figure when it came to emancipation.

Once again, the events of this year confirmed the power Toussaint held. General Rigaud and his forces in the southern province launched an all-out military offensive on Toussaint by attacking the town of Petit-Goâve. This marked the culmination of the rivalry between Toussaint and Rigaud, and it was Toussaint who would eventually emerge victorious.

Firstly, Toussaint and his men were technically engaged in a defensive effort, as Rigaud had struck first. Toussaint also acknowledged the rushed nature of the offensive from the south, realizing that it was motivated primarily by Rigaud's hatred toward him and a larger feud between the free people of color who supported Rigaud and his black supporters. In fact, Rigaud and his officers had clearly outlined their objective of replacing the white colonial rule of Saint-Domingue with a mixed-race elite, even if the black population of the island were granted full rights and liberties. And though Rigaud's forces were believed to be more disciplined, Toussaint's armies gained the upper hand after the intervention of their American friends. The US sent a navy to establish a blockade of the southern province and bombard the city of Jacmel, besieged by Toussaint's forces.

The conflict, known as the War of Knives, lasted for about a year, until the summer of 1800, and saw some of the bloodiest episodes of the Haitian Revolution. In addition to thousands of casualties directly from fighting, neither side preferred to take any prisoners, leading to the execution of thousands. Toussaint's commanders, Henri Christophe and Jean-Jacques Dessalines massacred those whom they suspected of being on Rigaud's side. Later, Toussaint would claim that he had not supported these crimes. Eventually outgunned and outmaneuvered, Rigaud and many of his officers fled Saint-Domingue, while many of their forces surrendered. By mid-1800, Toussaint had eliminated all his direct rivals in Saint-Domingue, though some, especially in the south, would remember the brutality of his forces and his cunning tactics in the years to come.

Louverturian Saint-Domingue

The nineteenth century began chaotically in France. The Directory was overthrown by Napoleon Bonaparte, who quickly introduced a new constitution and profoundly transformed the country and the global political climate over the next few years. In May 1804, when he declared himself emperor at Notre Dame, it seemed like France had gone full circle—back under the rule of a single monarch, just as it had been when the revolution began in 1789. By 1802, the dictatorial nature of his rule was already well apparent. In a fascinating turn of events, Napoleon invaded Saint-Domingue, still a French colony at the time, to overthrow Toussaint Louverture—a leader who had risen to prominence in a very similar way.

One-and-a-half years after Toussaint defeated Rigaud would mark the zenith of his power as the governor-general of French Saint-Domingue.

By the time his forces fought the French forces sent to the colony by Napoleon, he was, in every right, a dictator of Saint-Domingue. The measures that Toussaint adopted from 1800 to 1801 finally elevated him to the exalted status typical of a single ruler whose leadership inspires a mix of reverence and fear. In turn, these changes were only possible due to the black general's charismatic personality, past military achievements, and political skill, much like in the case of Napoleon.

Toussaint thus transformed the system in Saint-Domingue to guarantee he would keep the power he had accrued over the years. He was a war hero and a liberator of the black population of Saint-Domingue, which still constituted the majority. To gain the support of the local white and free colored people, on the other hand, he made sure to appoint them to the leading civil positions in his version of the colony's administration.

Toussaint insisted on racial equality, but his actions slowly made it clear that he intended to separate himself and his most ardent supporters from the rest of the black population. The highest-ranking officers in his armies were former black slaves whose loyalty Toussaint recognized by granting them large estates from his early days as governor. In turn, his officers never hesitated to follow their leader and allowed Toussaint to exercise a strict military regime over the population of Saint-Domingue. This sort of governance was necessary to keep the people in check, and he introduced some very firm laws.

Toussaint, claiming to adhere to the revolutionary principles of equality and liberty, nevertheless acted and reformed in a way that went around these ideals when needed. We have already discussed his support of Catholicism as the religion of Saint-Domingue, a radical break from revolutionary France. In addition to this, Toussaint had a clear vision for the future of Saint-Domingue that he believed rested on agricultural production as the basis of the colony's wealth and social structures.

In fact, Toussaint introduced a range of labor regulations in the fall of 1800, which asserted that liberty did not mean the people of Saint-Domingue could choose not to work, as then they would have nothing to contribute to society. Everyone was thus compelled to work in different industries, but agricultural labor was especially encouraged. Those who did not have another profession were expected to work in the fields. Rural parents were to ensure their children got used to field labor from a young age, even if it meant not sending their kids to school in the towns.

With these changes, the agricultural output of sugar and coffee in Saint-Domingue considerably increased according to official statistics in 1801. Toussaint's loyal and quite sizeable military allowed him to enforce these strict laws upon the population.

Toussaint also altered his behavior to assert his superiority over his direct subordinates and the rest of the population. Contemporary writings (mostly written by white colonists) state that Toussaint was a very charismatic person who was constantly on the move to make his presence known. He never ceased learning and had become quite a statesman, often directly addressing the public and not shying away from contact with commoners. He made it clear that he was to be respected, and people seemed to respect him wherever he went.

This was true for the Catholic clergy as well, with Toussaint sometimes even interfering in their sermons. He also regularly met with the white colonists, who needed Toussaint in order to run their plantations again. However, the black leader would often outsmart his visitors who had come to see him in hopes that he would affirm their wants or impose his authority to get what he wanted out of them, leaving his visitors embarrassed.

Importantly, Toussaint became out of touch with the black population, which came to significantly dislike him because of the strict labor laws and his demeanor, which they thought was disrespectful. The governor-general often publicly criticized and half-jokingly embarrassed the underprivileged black citizens of Saint-Domingue, for example, which did not resonate well with most of the population.

Two Dictators

By early 1800, Toussaint thus found himself in a peculiar position. He had risen to prominence because of his charismatic and unpredictable actions but had also grown more unpopular as he eliminated his political opponents in Saint-Domingue. What did not help his reputation was the attitude of the republicans back in France, who did not like the independent nature of Toussaint's actions. Especially after the overthrow of the Directory in 1799, there were increasingly more critics of Toussaint in the French political landscape. Some were his former allies from the Society of the Friends of the Blacks, who had initially supported his drive for emancipation.

The overthrow of the Directory signaled a change in colonial policy by the new French government, reorganized into a consulate by Napoleon, with the new Constitution of the Year VIII adopted very quickly in December 1799. Napoleon's regime was far more conservative than its predecessor, with Napoleon as the First Consul who had virtually all the power. Publicly, Napoleon and his allies said they supported the people of Saint-Domingue's full equality, but they also reminded the colony that it should have thanked Mother France for its liberty.

Toussaint, however, proclaimed to his supporters that emancipation had only been possible because of victory after years of fighting. He asserted that, had the people of Saint-Domingue not been strong enough, slavery would still be practiced, as was the case in other French colonies.

Though it is unclear whether it was Napoleon's initial objective to restore slavery in all of France's colonies, it was nevertheless apparent that Toussaint now regarded him as a rival. The relationship between them was far more complicated than what the black general believed, however. For the next few years, Toussaint sent many letters to Napoleon and his government, but he was disappointed when he received no answer. Toussaint was hopeful that a conservative regime in France support him if the motherland felt the economic effects of Saint-Domingue's revival. He deeply believed that he had done a lot for the colony and France and probably missed the recognition he had received in past years. Despite this, Napoleon never really saw Toussaint as his equal. It is possible Toussaint's future actions were directed to earn more respect from the First Consul of France, with whom he shared many similarities.

In January 1801, Toussaint thus sent a force of 20,000 to assert his control over the eastern part of Hispaniola, the formerly Spanish colony of Santo Domingo. Though this territory had been ceded to France, Commissioner Roume from the Third Civil Commission had failed to properly integrate it under French rule. Many Spanish authorities from the former colonial government were still in charge of different offices, and the French government had not taken any direct measures to change this. One reason behind this may have been that Paris was waiting for things to die down in Saint-Domingue before trying to bring Santo Domingo, which was far less valuable than the western part of the island, under its firmer rule.

Thus, Toussaint's forces, commanded by his loyal adopted nephew, General Moïse, easily walked their way into Santo Domingo, claiming it in the name of France. Toussaint declared that he intended to fully modernize the eastern part of the island, which had been underdeveloped in the hands of the Spanish, and build an egalitarian society just as he had done in Saint-Domingue. This was positively received by the underprivileged black majority of its population.

Toussaint's actions spelled a clear break from the French government, as he had acted completely by himself and had gone against the wishes of Paris. The black general notified Napoleon of his actions only after the takeover of the colony, stating that he had emancipated Santo Domingo. He received no reply.

If this was not enough, Toussaint also proceeded to issue his own constitution for Saint-Domingue, an unprecedented move that further proved to Napoleon that he must assert central authority over the black general. Toussaint's document was drawn up in the spring of 1801 by a specially-created committee of white and mixed-race members, appointed by the black general. It was, of course, modeled after the many constitutions of revolutionary France, and its first article asserted that Saint-Domingue was part of the French Empire. Toussaint's constitution also guaranteed equal liberties and full rights to men of all races in the colony, which now included the whole island of Hispaniola. Slavery was to remain abolished, and civil and military positions were to be open to members of all races and classes.

It was far from a democratic document, however, instead representing a "legal" basis for establishing a dictatorship in Saint-Domingue. Saint-Domingue's constitution declared Toussaint governor-general for life, with virtually unlimited power that included the appointment and dismissal of civil and military officials. A legal assembly was also to be introduced, which would vote to pass laws proposed by Toussaint but have no authority to introduce new laws itself. The assembly was to be comprised of members chosen by the governors, who, in turn, were appointed by Toussaint. It also made Catholicism the only official religion of Saint-Domingue, outlawing all other religious practices.

Despite their liberties being guaranteed by the constitution, the people of Saint-Domingue were prohibited from engaging in political activities by forming political society groups. The government had the right to arrest anyone it suspected of being involved in such practices.

The constitution also asserted the importance of property rights, a move that guaranteed that the wealthier plantation owners, often allies of Toussaint, would retain their extensive estates, with their interests defended by the government.

Toussaint's constitution, which was promulgated in July 1801, radically transformed the social and political structure of Saint-Domingue and the colony's relationship with Paris. Toussaint Louverture was now the dictator of Saint-Domingue and had a constitutionally guaranteed right to keep his position until his death. In fact, Toussaint declared himself ruler for life one year before Napoleon did, with his new constitution of 1802.

In hindsight, the adoption of the constitution and such a clear break from France would prove to be a hasty move, resulting in Napoleon sending an army to restore French authority in the colony. For Napoleon, Toussaint was just another arrogant leader who assigned more importance to himself than he deserved, and he was to be quickly punished for it.

Whatever the case may be, Toussaint underestimated the response from Paris, which had long had far more immediate issues to deal with. He also underestimated the international situation by the time the constitution was published, as France had stopped its Quasi-War with the United States. The US's newly elected slave-owning president, Thomas Jefferson, was less likely to support him than his predecessor John Adams' administration had in the past. France was also on its way to normalizing its relations with Britain, which would allow Napoleon to send his forces to Saint-Domingue without the threat of the British Royal Navy. The stage was now set for a full-scale escalation between the two dictators.

Chapter Five – The Birth of Haiti

In this chapter, we will examine the downfall of Toussaint Louverture—the man who, looking up to Napoleon, had declared himself governor-general of Saint-Domingue for life. As we will see, Toussaint's ambitions would not go unnoticed in Paris, where Napoleon's conservative government held dubious feelings about such an unpredictable figure. Toussaint's rise to power would eventually prompt Napoleon to send a sizeable force led by one of his most experienced generals to reestablish firm French control over the colony. Despite the defeat of the black governor-general, the French would be unable to maintain their control over Saint-Domingue for long. Other black leaders of the revolution, most prominently Jean-Jacques Dessalines, would resist the return of a brutal colonial regime. At this crucial moment, the Republic of Haiti as an independent nation would be born.

French Invasion of Saint-Domingue

The Haitian Revolution began in 1791 and lasted for over a decade, ending in 1804 with the proclamation of Haiti's independence. However, the short period from early 1802 to late 1803 was by far the most violent part of the conflict, which saw an escalation on a level previously unseen in Saint-Domingue.

We have already mentioned that by the time Toussaint Louverture issued a separate constitution for the colony of Saint-Domingue, claiming the position of governor-general for life, First Consul Napoleon Bonaparte had already been planning to send forces to Saint-Domingue. The political landscape in France at the time was chaotic, and several different circumstances may have played a role in Napoleon's decision to launch a large-scale invasion of the colony.

Though pro-slavery sentiments in France had significantly increased since Napoleon's coming to power, some still advocated for allying with Louverture, believing it was the only way to retain Saint-Domingue as a profitable colony. Napoleon, however, took no advice from his subordinates. His decision to invade Saint-Domingue was final, partly motivated by the arrogance of Toussaint. At the time, France had the most professional army, which had successfully fought the other European powers for many years.

The French ruler was confident in the correctness of his decision. Napoleon envisioned a vast French Empire that was the center and the model of European civilization and believed that the wealth flowing in from the colonies was an essential part of his vision. Thus, he did not want to give up Saint-Domingue. After getting rid of Toussaint, he preferred to reestablish firmer French control, much like there had been before the insurrection.

He chose an experienced commander and the husband of his sister, General Charles Victor Emmanuel Leclerc, to lead the expedition and reclaim the colony. Leclerc had been an early ally of Napoleon, taking part both in the Italian campaign and the coup that had brought the latter to power, and thus was greatly trusted by the soon-to-be emperor. Leclerc would lead a sizeable force of 20,000 men, tasked with taking control of Saint-Domingue, disarming the black population, and establishing strict white military control, with Toussaint and other leading men of color arrested and sent to France.

In addition to the force that was comprised of experienced veterans from France's European wars, the armada that Napoleon assembled to sail to Saint-Domingue also carried old political rivals of Toussaint Louverture—André Rigaud and Alexandre Pétion, who had led the free people of color's resistance in the southern province. Toussaint's two sons, whom he had sent to France to be educated six years earlier, were also returned. They carried a letter that called Toussaint to accept the authority of General Leclerc and surrender control of the colony without bloody fighting.

The expedition was to land in Santo Domingo (the formerly Spanish part of the island) and slowly work its way through to the domains best controlled by Toussaint. Somewhat unexpectedly, the fleet had to delay departure from France until December 1801, which meant the forces had less time to complete their mission before the coming of summer, which would bring harsh climate conditions and tropical diseases to the unaccustomed French. Nevertheless, hopes were high that the experienced and numerous French would quickly be able to subdue the rogue black general.

In early 1802, some forces landed in Santo Domingo, while most of the army was transported by ships to the north, where they landed in early February 1803. Just east of Cap-Français, they attacked the settlement of Fort Liberté, easily taking it from the black defenders, who were outnumbered. After the takeover, the French army massacred the surviving black garrison in one of the first acts of brutality that would become a staple of the war for the next few years.

Despite its forces suffering defeat in the first encounter, Saint-Domingue was nevertheless very well defended. This was a side effect of years of fighting, which had given valuable experience to most of the black soldiers enlisted in Toussaint's army. The colony's population was used to war, and many of them had successfully defeated European forces before. People in the countryside were well armed and had superior knowledge of the terrain, giving them a natural advantage as they organized their defense. The officers tasked with directing the population when the fighting broke out were ordered to burn the plantations as they retreated to the cities. Toussaint wanted to avoid a direct confrontation with the French army and fully utilized his defensive head start. Le Cap and Port-au-Prince were the main centers of resistance where most of Toussaint's forces were concentrated.

The main problem Toussaint Louverture faced was the question of whether the people of Saint-Domingue would take up arms and follow his lead. After he had established himself as a dictator, much of the population was upset with the harsh policies he had implemented. They acknowledged that Toussaint had led them to freedom, but not many had seen an improvement in their living standards after emancipation, an improvement they knew was possible. Black citizens, most of whom had become subsistence farmers after the abolition of slavery, were resentful toward more privileged white people, black people, and people of color they believed constantly looked down on them. In addition, many white people and people of color would gladly see the end of Toussaint's dictatorship. They had recently learned that Toussaint was capable of getting rid of anyone he suspected of being his enemy. He had executed his nephew, the formerly trusted General Moïse, in 1801 after the latter had disagreed with Toussaint over his adoption of the constitution.

The French took over Santo Domingo without much fighting. Toussaint's generals assigned there quickly submitted to the invaders. So did General Jean Laplume, commander of Saint-Domingue's forces in the south, where the population of white people and people of color was the least supportive of Toussaint Louverture after the incidents of the War of Knives.

General Henri Christophe was in charge of defending Cap-Français, where French General Leclerc led the troops himself. Christophe's determination to defend the city can be seen in the letters exchanged between the two generals. After Christophe refused to surrender, the French armada began a heavy bombardment of Cap-Français and made its way into the harbor. Christophe, realizing he was outgunned, abandoned the city and took his forces to the countryside, setting up in the mountains.

In the west, General Dessalines was similarly forced to retreat from Port-au-Prince after putting up a strong resistance against the French. Many white and mixed-race soldiers of Dessalines' force deserted the black general, switching allegiance to the French, which further weakened his position. As he also retreated to the mountains, Dessalines spread the word that the French intended to reinstitute slavery and set fire to many villages and plantations on his way. He also ordered his troops to kill hundreds of white inhabitants of the countryside.

As his main forces were retreating from the cities and ceding them to the French, Toussaint urged the rural population of Saint-Domingue to rise up and fight for their freedom.

In addition to the organized resistance of Toussaint's generals, there were, in fact, several guerilla fighting squads that were a thorn in the side of the French armies. It is unclear, however, whether these fighters saw Toussaint as their leader or had decided to resist the invasion by themselves.

Meanwhile, General Leclerc failed to convince Toussaint to surrender and declared him an outlaw in February. Disappointed by the unsuccessful negotiations, Leclerc ordered his most elite corps, commanded by General Rochambeau, to surround the resisting armies of Dessalines and Toussaint in the mountains that separated the northern and western provinces.

On February 23, Toussaint led his forces at the Battle of Ravine-à-Couleuvres, where he managed to hold off the French advance for six hours. Eventually, however, after both sides suffered heavy casualties, he ordered his men to retreat.

The French then advanced to attack Crête-à-Pierrot, an old British fort that was being defended by Dessalines and his men. Both sides acknowledged the importance of holding Crête-à-Pierrot, as it was located in a strategic position, and fierce fighting continued until the end of March. Dessalines was outgunned once again but made a valiant effort to defend the fort. The accounts of Dessalines' resistance come from a captured French physicist, Michel Descourtilz, who remarked on the black general's strength of character and ability to inspire his troops even as the battle seemed lost. Eventually, Dessalines had to give up his position, but he promised his men he would never give up fighting. The defense of Crête-à-Pierrot was later considered a heroic episode of the war and a fundamental part of Haitian national identity.

Attack and take of Crête-à-Pierrot by Auguste Raffet.
https://commons.wikimedia.org/wiki/File:Haitian_Revolution.jpg

Despite the resistance, the French were too much for Toussaint and his armies to deal with. The French were overwhelming the defenders and massacring black people suspected of supporting Toussaint. The fact that the war was essentially lost became more evident when by early May, all of Toussaint's generals had either surrendered or switched sides to the French. Leclerc promised to pardon and grant military and civil offices to Christophe and Dessalines, a promise he upheld.

The surrender of his generals forced Toussaint to give up, as well. In early May, he appeared before Leclerc in Cap-Français with an escort of a few hundred men and publicly recognized the French general's authority. Leclerc, despite his negative sentiments toward the black general, decided to grant Toussaint a plantation at Ennery, east of the coastal city of Gonaïves, where he expected him to retire peacefully and cause no further disturbance as he consolidated his position as the new governor of Saint-Domingue.

On May 7, Leclerc wrote a letter to Napoleon in which he declared victory and remarked that all the leaders of the resistance had been pacified. A month later, however, recognizing the constant threat that Toussaint's presence posed to his authority, Leclerc had him arrested at his estate and sent to Gonaïves, where he was shipped to France. Toussaint Louverture, a slave-turned-leader-turned-dictator, died in solitary imprisonment the next year (April 1803) in the remote French prison of Fort de Joux, thousands of miles away from Saint-Domingue, where he had successfully led one of the biggest slave uprisings in history.

Resistance Continues

By the summer of 1803, Leclerc sought to reestablish firm central control over Saint-Domingue, which was still a colony of Napoleon's France. The renewed military operations had once again disturbed the colony's economic output, which was still of major importance to Paris. With the black generals on his side, Leclerc believed that a well-organized resistance from the black population was impossible.

However, the situation in Saint-Domingue had not at all been pacified to the extent that the French general claimed. Rural black residents, who had reorganized into guerilla fighting squads, still posed a significant threat to the French forces on the island, launching unexpected small-scale attacks of great intensity on the French soldiers. The black population of the island was determined to defend its freedom at all costs and by no means supported the reimposition of French authority.

Leclerc was aware of this. One of the reasons he had arrested Toussaint was that he believed the black general would soon incite a rebellion against him. But by the time Toussaint was arrested, war and disease had taken their toll on the French. Over 8,000 men from the initial expedition of 20,000 were killed, and in the summer, the tropical diseases claimed the lives of increasingly more of Leclerc's white fighters. Undersupplied and undermanned, Leclerc decided not to spread his forces too thin and assert his power in the countryside. He could not afford to suffer more unnecessary casualties. Instead, he awaited support from Paris.

Soon after the takeover of Saint-Domingue, the French general voiced his intention to disarm the rural population. Though his white forces were in no shape to enforce this measure, the black generals who had switched sides to support the French were more than ready to carry out Leclerc's orders. Henry Christophe and Jean-Jacques Dessalines led the mostly black forces loyal to them against the guerilla militants, most of whom were also black. Often, they brutally pursued the rebels. Dessalines was especially infamous for showing no mercy.

Despite this, Leclerc knew that he could not rely too heavily on the black generals. His intent was never to treat the black and mixed-race people of the colony as equals to the white French. For example, he did not allow Creole men to hold civil positions and encouraged violence between Saint-Domingue's urban people of color. To ensure people of mixed race would not pose a significant threat to his position, Leclerc sent André Rigaud, the old rival of Toussaint, back to France in May 1803.

Thus, even after the defeat of Toussaint, Saint-Domingue was not at all under firm French control. The situation would become more complicated after Napoleon's government officially repealed the 1794 law about the abolition of slavery. Napoleon also authorized the practice of slavery in French colonies where it had never been repealed, thus strengthening the position of French colonists in places like Martinique. The new decree was followed by a general increase in anti-black sentiments in French cities.

The news of Napoleon's decision would reach Saint-Domingue in August, and it is not hard to guess why it would lead to a widespread denouncement of the French policy. Though the law did not technically affect the situation in Saint-Domingue, the black population of the colony was concerned that slavery, with all its grim practices, would be re-established. They were not about to give up their liberties after more than ten years of fighting for them. One by one, the black officers loyal to Leclerc thus began to desert him. Alexandre Pétion, one of the leaders of the mixed-race forces during the War of Knives, declared in October that he was back on the black insurgents' side. So did Jean-Jacques Dessalines and Henri Christophe.

Fearing that the black population of Le Cap would join the rebels, General Leclerc, who had contracted yellow fever, ordered the execution of the city's black garrison. Over a thousand of Leclerc's black soldiers were thus drowned by white officers in the harbor of Cap-Français.

Leclerc wrote to Napoleon that the black resistance was gaining momentum, in hopes of more reinforcements. But the reinforcements that had arrived from Europe a few months before also suffered from yellow fever.

Moreover, some Polish legions, who had served in Napoleon's armies since the Third Partition of Poland and had been sent to Saint-Domingue to support Leclerc, deserted the French and sided with the insurgents. The Poles had been told they were being sent to the colony to suppress a rebellion, but they realized the true nature of French oppression upon their arrival. Poles who remained among the French forces deliberately did not massacre the black fighters when they were ordered to by their superiors. Famously, after the independence of Haiti, Dessalines recognized the support the black people had gotten from the Poles, granting those who remained in the colony Haitian citizenship and full legal rights. He believed that Poles were the "white [blacks] of Europe," emphasizing the similar nature of their struggles.

Leclerc died soon after contracting yellow fever, in the late fall of 1802. General Rochambeau, the second-in-command, assumed leadership of the French. The scale of the violence increased as French white and black populations of Saint-Domingue relentlessly massacred each other over the following months. Thousands more were reduced to extreme poverty, their houses and small farms burned. What progress the colony had undergone during the small period of peace was quickly being undermined. This only caused the resentment of the French to grow.

The Defeat of the French

Though the French managed to stabilize the situation a bit throughout the winter, the resistance movement was significantly growing each day, and Jean-Jacques Dessalines was emerging as its main leader. Dessalines was the new figure around whom the non-white population of Saint-Domingue began to assemble—even mixed-race colonists who had been against the complete equality of the three racial groups. This was one way the new leader was different from Toussaint Louverture, from whom he had certainly learned a lot.

The stark contrast between the two was that Toussaint had always considered the possibility of making peace with the French. His Saint-Domingue would be a proud colony of Mother France, with equality between the races and no more slavery but a clearly defined white and mixed-race elite. Dessalines' vision was radically different. He had no intention of reconciling with the French from the beginning. He fully believed it was in the interests of France to reinstate slavery in Saint-Domingue, and he could not allow that to happen. He saw the war as a struggle between the French and their colonial interests on one side and the black and mixed-race population on the other.

It can be assumed that this stemmed from Dessalines' background, which had been very different from Toussaint's. Unlike Toussaint, Dessalines had still been a slave when the uprising broke out in 1791. Dessalines had been forged in the rebellion and had naturally become its leader.

The clear break from a French identity in favor of a united mixed-race and black front was expressed by the rebels with their adoption of a new flag. Instead of the revolutionary French tricolor, the new flag was comprised of black stripes, signaling the union between the two groups of the colony. It was clear that Dessalines was leading a new independence movement, different from Toussaint's.

Jean-Jacques Dessalines by Louis Rigaud.
https://commons.wikimedia.org/wiki/File:Jean_Jacques_Dessalines.jpg

Meanwhile, in early 1803, France had once again entered into war with Great Britain. This caused huge complications in the conflict in Saint-Domingue. Napoleon knew he did not possess a strong enough navy to maintain his colonial empire in the Caribbean. The British would not allow the French to send reinforcements to its colonies, which might pose a threat to their own in the New World. Napoleon also recognized that he had underestimated the resistance that the people of Saint-Domingue could put up and knew that the fight for the colony was lost. Thus, the French leader soon decided it would be better to abandon the New World possessions of France and fully focus on expansion in Europe.

A clear indication of this shift was the famous Louisiana Purchase of 1803, in which Napoleon sold the huge French territory of Louisiana—more than 800,000 square miles in size—to the United States for fifteen million dollars. This money would be used to finance Napoleon's future military campaigns, and the sale of the huge colony to the United States meant the British would be unable to take it for themselves.

Saint-Domingue, on the other hand, was abandoned. Soon after the declaration of war between France and Britain in May 1803, British ships began to blockade the colony's ports and lent their support to the rebels against the French colonies. The colonial undertakings of Napoleon had proven to be a disaster. Were it not for his decisive victories in Europe and the strict censorship of the French press, it is likely that the defeat of French forces in the Caribbean would have caused public outrage.

General Rochambeau, the new leader of the French forces in Saint-Domingue, realized he could not retain control over the colony. He resorted to extreme measures that first included massacring the captured black rebels, then civilians, and finally innocent women and children. The French general also resented people of mixed race. He believed that they were fundamentally different from white people and rejected the idea that the two groups were similar when it came to privilege, for example.

Perhaps Rochambeau knew that his decision to massacre the mixed-race population of Saint-Domingue would not bring victory. Contemporary records mention that life in Cap-Français had a strange atmosphere, with the white population of the city acknowledging that the French were doomed to defeat.

Dessalines and his men, on the other hand, responded to the brutal measures of the French by massacring hundreds of white people, killing many of the wealthy planters who had regained their estates after the Toussaint's victory. In October, Dessalines' forces took Port-au-Prince and brutally massacred hundreds of white people in the city. In November, his forces promptly defeated the final resistance of the French just outside of Le Cap, in the Battle of Vertières.

General Rochambeau, who realized that defeat was inevitable, surrendered the remainder of his forces in Port-au-Prince to the British navy that had been blockading the harbor. The French general preferred to be imprisoned by the British rather than surrender to Dessalines. By late November, the fight for Saint-Domingue was over.

Haiti

On January 1, 1804, Jean-Jacques Dessalines declared the independence of the people of Saint-Domingue. The name given to the newly independent country was Haiti (or Ayiti), derived from the Taino language of the indigenous Arawak peoples of Hispaniola. "Haiti" was the word they had used to refer to the island, meaning "land of high mountains." The adoption of the name was a conscious break with the country's colonial past and an identification with Hispaniola's original inhabitants.

The Haitian Declaration of Independence was only the second of such documents after the US Declaration of Independence in 1776. The document asserted that France remained an enemy despite the victory of the Haitian people and recognized the atrocities France had committed during colonial occupation. This was followed by a written constitution a year later, in 1805. The new Haitian constitution was very compelling, to say the least. Just like Toussaint's constitution four years earlier, it asserted that slavery was forever abolished in Haiti, making it the first constitutional document in the world to say so. It also made Dessalines emperor for life with the name Jacques I, a decision that was inspired by the crowning of Napoleon as emperor a few months before. The constitution gave full citizenship to all men regardless of their race but prohibited white people from acquiring property in Haiti, a measure that was taken to prevent the old planters from returning.

However, asserting full equality between the races did not erase the memory of Dessalines' brutalities against the white population in colonial Saint-Domingue. He had already done a lot to show that he did not intend Haiti to be a state for whites. In addition to killing thousands of white French during the war, Dessalines proceeded to execute hundreds more who had surrendered to him after the defeat of Rochambeau. Throughout the spring of 1804, he traveled from city to city to personally ensure that the rest of the white colonists were stripped of their property, arrested, and executed. This incident, which became known as the Haitian Genocide, resulted in the death of up to 5,000 people, and the almost full elimination of Haiti's white population.

In the eyes of Dessalines, the killings were justified. The white residents were paying with their lives the cost of the damages caused by the colonists. It was a genocidal act of revenge against the white French of Haiti, even as Dessalines sought to normalize relations with other white nations and groups within the country. In addition to sparing the lives of the Polish who switched sides during the war, he also spared a small group of German colonists in the northwestern region who had lived in the area before 1791. Select white men who held important professions, such as doctors, were also not executed. As for other nations, Dessalines was happy to engage in trade relations with the British and the Americans, aware of their support during the revolution. The Haitian Genocide showed Dessalines' intent to rule with full brutal authority and his readiness to have innocents executed. It was remarked that he often made those who were reluctant to shoot the white residents take part in executions. This was even true of the mixed-race population, as Dessalines insisted that they should no longer identify at all with the white population.

It is not difficult to guess that the new constitution was specifically designed by Dessalines to give him unlimited power. This was already clear from his proclamation as emperor for life. Unlike Toussaint's constitution, no legislative body was created to act even as a façade of a countermeasure against the emperor's authority. Dessalines had full power to raise armies, issue laws, and collect taxes, making him a textbook dictator. In some regards, the new constitution continued the authoritarian legacy of Toussaint's document of 1801, especially regarding the creation of a militarized society.

The population of the newly independent Haitian Empire was by no means free. The document did not assert their rights to assembly or freedom of the press. It did assert that Haitians were expected to be law-abiding citizens or they would suffer the harsh consequences. All in all, the fact that Haiti now had a constitution did not mean that it was reorganized into a democratic state, though contemporary records of white merchants that visited its ports mentioned that the new country functioned surprisingly better than what was expected of a black society. Though the Haitian Revolution was over, after thirteen years of constant and brutal fighting, the next few years would play as much of an important role.

Chapter Six – Aftermath

In the concluding chapter of the book, we will look at the events that transpired in Haiti after Dessalines proclaimed independence in 1804. We will look at the regime that Dessalines imposed on his subjects, one that was not far from the dictatorship of Toussaint Louverture. We will examine what caused the young Haitian republic to split into two rival parts about two years after it gained its sovereignty and how its leaders confronted the many national and international challenges in the first few decades after independence. Finally, we will explore the short and long-term consequences of the Haitian Revolution and its far-reaching legacy that still makes it as relevant as ever in the twenty-first century.

Post-Revolutionary Haiti

For those unfamiliar with the history of colonialism, it is perhaps easy to imagine the birth of a stable nation after the fight with a colonial power. This conception may come from the case of the United States, arguably the most prominent example of a new nation successfully transitioning to independence after years of colonial rule. However, this is not usually the case. Even the United States had to face many immediate problems after gaining independence in 1783. It fought several more wars against its former colonial ruler, including one in 1812, that certainly took a toll on the young American nation.

The proclamation of independence is hardly ever the end of the perilous situation that exists in a post-colonial nation. For many countries, as would especially be the case in underdeveloped Africa and South America, the period immediately after the end of colonial rule shapes their identity and distinguishes them from neighboring countries. The main problem lies in the fact that few newly independent countries have the resources and experience to properly govern themselves. Sometimes, the leaders who led the nation during the revolution don't exactly garner the same support once they take control of the former colony. A more profound problem that arises is the lack of a sense of purpose or an objective. During colonial rule, it is easier to unite the colonized under a collective motive. It is easier to display the colonial power as an unjust oppressor who must be overthrown and proclaim that liberty must be achieved at all costs. It becomes more difficult when the new nation, independent of colonial rule, must define what exactly this liberty means and set up new institutions. In 1805, Haiti had to face all these problems.

It is an understatement to say that the situation in post-revolutionary Haiti was chaotic. General Dessalines, now Emperor Jacques I, had directly adopted the worst aspects from Louverturian Saint-Domingue of 1801. The new constitution granted him even more power than the old one had granted to Toussaint, and, in many regards, Dessalines would walk the path of his predecessor.

Just like after the first expulsion of the French, Dessalines claimed that the restoration of economic activity was his main motivation. Still, as the lands were redistributed to black Haitians, many remained subject to the strict labor regulations initially introduced by Toussaint. In turn, these had been modifications of the old plantation system that existed with slavery. Most of Haiti's population was still very poor in 1805, and it did not help that most of the country had been destroyed during the revolution. In the mountainous countryside, for example, the lack of road maintenance meant that most were unfit to be used by carriages; in turn, this meant there were problems with interconnectivity. Some agricultural projects that had been carried out by the French, like irrigation systems in the mountains that provided water to the sugar plantations, were also destroyed, significantly affecting production in those areas.

Infrastructural and administrative problems added to the demographic catastrophe that Haiti had struggled with since the beginning of the revolution in 1791. While it is difficult to calculate the exact casualty rate, we know that the population in 1804 was about 300,000 and that the colony had more women than men, a sign of the destructive nature of the conflict. Moreover, long were gone the colonial days when thousands of new slaves would be brought from Africa to bolster the population.

Unfortunately for the Haitians, the independence of their nation coincided with the rise of imperialist and racist attitudes in nineteenth-century Europe, which quickly spread throughout the world. Haiti was the first example of a free black society in the modern world, and many doubted that the new nation could continue its existence for a long time. While outside interference and the reassertion of French control seemed unlikely while the British ruled the Caribbean basin, France refused to recognize Haitian independence for years. Sentiments about reclaiming France's lost Caribbean possessions certainly persevered among the higher echelons of French society when Napoleon's European victories made the French Empire the most feared power on the continent.

The only immediate external threat to Haiti was the eastern part of Hispaniola, where a remnant of French resistance under French General Jean-Louis Ferrand had refused to surrender to Dessalines by 1805. In February, after believing that he had sufficiently consolidated his power, the Haitian emperor thus launched his invasion of Santo Domingo.

If anything, Dessalines' invasion of Santo Domingo was a precautionary measure in hopes that it would bring a quick victory and avoid a potential French invasion from the east. In hindsight, however, it proved to be a rushed move that spelled the doom of the Haitian emperor, who never possessed the political skill of his predecessor, Toussaint.

French General Ferrand had imposed strict white control over Santo Domingo and practiced slavery, supported by the old white Spanish landowners. There were just over 20,000 slaves in Santo Domingo at the time of Dessalines' invasion, but, contrary to what he expected, they did not rise up to support him.

The reason for this was the distinct cultural and historical circumstances behind the practice of slavery in Spanish Santo Domingo versus its practice in French Saint-Domingue. Black slaves in the Spanish part of the island, though still subject to harsh rule, had much more freedom than had been enjoyed by the slaves in the French part of Hispaniola. In addition, they were aware that the abolition of slavery in Haiti had not exactly brought prosperity to the Haitian black population and had heard of the strict labor system that had been put in place, first by Toussaint and then by Dessalines.

Without their support, Dessalines' invasion was certainly a rash endeavor. But as the Haitian forces laid siege to the city of Santo Domingo, they noticed the arrival of some French warships that dissuaded them from continuing their assault. Dessalines and his generals retreated, devastating the countryside on their way back to Haiti and massacring and imprisoning hundreds of people. The French, led by Ferrand, would remain in control of Santo Domingo until 1809.

The failure to take Santo Domingo was Dessalines' first major mistake. As Toussaint's record shows, if one claims to rule for all but rules by fear, one cannot be allowed to make mistakes. Toussaint did not necessarily fail in any of the endeavors he undertook during his time as governor-general of Saint-Domingue. He underestimated the strength and the will of the French to reinvade the island and overthrow him. Dessalines, with his failed campaign, showed that he had not learned from the faults of his predecessor. In his case, his demise was caused from the inside rather than an external invasion.

As mentioned, leading a colonized nation during a revolution does not imply that the leader is apt when it comes to governance. Dessalines was such a leader. His ascent to power owed a lot to chance and being in the right place at the right time, in addition to his military successes. It was clear that his policies would lead the black majority of the Haitian population nowhere. The military control that was imposed on the black farmers was becoming stricter in hopes that it would boost production. If that was not enough, Dessalines had significant conflicts with mixed-race members of the elite, whose privileges he constantly threatened and undermined. Many of his soldiers also were not comfortable following the brutal orders of their leader. Thus, Dessalines had managed to upset a large portion of his followers who had previously supported him as a new liberator and peacemaker.

Following the defeat at Santo Domingo, Alexandre Pétion organized a conspiracy against the emperor in 1806, which was joined by many of Dessalines' generals, including Henri Christophe. Their declared goal was to end Dessalines' brutal dictatorship and improve the conditions of different interest groups. In October 1806, the conspirators assassinated him, though the exact way Dessalines' death took place remains uncertain. According to one account, Dessalines was ambushed on his way to Port-au-Prince and shot twice. His body was taken to the city and paraded in front of thousands who had assembled to see the dead tyrant. Then, it was torn apart by the crowd and left at the public square. The remains were later gathered by a black woman and buried.

Two Haitis

Dessalines' assassination marked the beginning of a new era in the history of young Haiti. This new era, however, did not bring about the changes many Haitians so desperately needed to improve their living conditions after years of fighting. Instead, the conspirators who had gotten rid of Dessalines were unable to keep the country unified. The only similarity that the leading generals of the coup shared was their hatred toward the French and the dictatorial regime of Dessalines, and they soon quarreled over how exactly they wanted to reorganize Haiti in 1806.

Henri Christophe, the second man in Haiti before the assassination of Dessalines, regarded himself as the logical successor to the late emperor, though perhaps not adopting the same title. Alexandre Pétion and his supporters, on the other hand, believed Haiti should no longer be ruled by one person who held all the power. They drew up a new constitution that would make Christophe president but would drastically limit his powers in favor of a legislative assembly. Christophe rejected the proposal and abandoned Pétion, returning to Le Cap, where the base of his support was concentrated. There, he established his own government modeled after that of Dessalines, with a lot of power in his hands.

In the south, Pétion, supported by a small number of mixed-race elite, was elected as president in a governmental system that can best be described as an oligarchy, with select individuals possessing more power.

Henri Christophe by Richard Evans.
https://commons.wikimedia.org/wiki/File:Henri_Christophe.jpg

The northern part of Haiti, under Christophe, was at first called the State of Haiti. In 1811, it was reorganized into a kingdom, with Christophe becoming King Henry I.

The southern part was established, from the get-go, as the Republic of Haiti. There, too, Pétion, who held considerable influence over the members of his legislative assembly (the Senate), began to gain more and more power, which the assembly transferred to him over time. This culminated in him rewriting the constitution he had drawn up in 1806, proclaiming himself president for life in 1816.

Though it is easy to describe the split of 1806 as the continuation of a long-standing conflict between the black population of the north and the mixed-race population of the south, the new division was not strictly based on racial terms. Christophe, throughout his time as first the president and then the king, relied heavily on advice from his inner circle of mixed-race and even white advisors. On the other hand, while the mixed-race *anciens libres* held more wealth than the black residents in the south, the majority of the population in Pétion's republic were black farmers, and his army was mostly black, as well.

An armed conflict broke out between the two sides soon after the split of the former co-conspirators. Neither side launched large-scale invasions of the other's territory, though the small-scale raids were frequent, especially at the start.

The reasons for this are twofold. Firstly, the territories of each side after the split were not well defined. Secondly, both Pétion and Christophe had to deal with internal difficulties and resistance, including breakaway regions that would rebel and remain out of reach for the rulers for years. The international opinion on the two also varied significantly. As both rulers tried to gain support from the British in Jamaica, the British were content to see Haiti—an example of a successfully decolonized New World nation—remain destabilized and weak. Pétion and Christophe, seeing no prospects of quick reconciliation, thus began pursuing very different policies in their respective domains.

Christophe, who was crowned king in 1811 by the archbishop of Milot, Jean-Baptiste-Joseph Brelle, lived as a king in every aspect. For his coronation, he had lavish accessories and decorations imported from Britain, and he built multiple palaces and fortifications in the north throughout his reign. La Citadelle, for example, often called Citadelle Henri Christophe, is a marvelous fortress that was completed in 1820 after more than ten years of building. It is located atop a 3,000-foot-high hill at a strategic location south of Le Cap and still stands today as a prime example of the ambitious projects undertaken during Christophe's reign. It is estimated that over 20,000 black peasants were forced to work on the construction of La Citadelle, out of which at least 2,000 died at the site.

This fact is indicative of Christophe's continuation of the strict labor policies elaborated during Toussaint's and Dessalines' regimes. He still viewed agricultural production as the main savior of his kingdom's economy and believed that the best way to get the most out of Haitian lands was to keep the plantations concentrated in the hands of a small number of planters.

Differently from Christophe, Pétion broke up many of the large plantations and granted the lands to soldiers and struggling farmers. This move was designed to ensure that these groups did not feel oppressed, especially as the mixed-race *anciens libres* occupied the top offices.

However, Christophe undertook more measures when it came to giving basic education to most of his population. His contacts with the British (Christophe had been born in the British colony of Grenada) also led to an increase in trade and subsequent economic gains.

Meanwhile, significant political changes were happening in France, where the Bourbon monarchy was restored after the defeat of Napoleon in 1814. The conservative government of Louis XVIII, the brother of the guillotined Louis XVI, expressed a strong desire to reclaim control over Saint-Domingue —the old "Pearl of the Antilles." The independence of Haiti had still not been recognized by Paris. Discussion about returning to Saint-Domingue increased after Britain agreed to cede control over Martinique and Guadalupe to Bourbon France. In these colonies, slavery had been fully maintained by the British.

Aware of the long-standing social conflicts in Haiti, as well as the recent overthrow of Dessalines and the disunification of the new nation, many in the government believed that French control over Saint-Domingue could be re-established. The French tried to negotiate with members of the mixed-race elite in Haiti, hoping that they would be willing to help them reimpose control over Haiti and possibly even bring back the enslavement of the black population. This, however, was where every Haitian drew a line. The return of the French colonial regime, let alone the possible reinstatement of slavery, was out of the question for all Haitians, for the supporters of both Pétion and Christophe.

It was thus made clear that France's return to Haiti was out of the question. On the contrary, what many in the Haitian governments wanted was for France to recognize the new nation as a fully sovereign country. Official recognition from France would lead to the normalization of relations and would help Haiti progress economically, as trade would open up. Pétion's followers expressed this sentiment more than the followers of Christophe, as the Kingdom of Haiti of Henry I had already established close trade relations with the British.

Ultimately, neither leader would live long enough to see Haiti reunited, let alone recognized by France. Pétion died in 1818, just two years after proclaiming himself president for life. Jean-Pierre Boyer, another veteran of the revolution, had been chosen by Pétion himself as his successor.

Soon after becoming president, Boyer was presented with an opportunity to reunite the north and south: to everyone's surprise, Christophe committed suicide in 1820. The king's health had declined immensely after he suffered a stroke earlier that year, making him unable to oversee his realm. Afraid of the growing resentful sentiments of his population, who viewed Christophe as just another brutal dictator, Christophe shot himself in his royal palace at Sans-Souci. Boyer, having heard of the death of his northern rival, was quick to assemble his forces and claim the former kingdom for himself, thus uniting the country in late 1820.

Two years later, in 1822, President Boyer annexed Spanish Santo Domingo, thus uniting Hispaniola under Haitian rule. Chaos had unfolded in Santo Domingo after Dessalines' failed invasion in 1805. The colony had only remained under French control until the 1808 outbreak of war between Napoleonic France and Spain in Europe. The Spanish soon sent an invasion force that quickly defeated the small French resistance in Santo Domingo and easily reestablished control over the colony, supported by most of the population, which preferred Spanish rule over that of the French. The Spanish government, however, exercised little control over the colony, and the wealthy Spanish white colonists continued to practice slavery, something that turned the population against them.

After Boyer had come to power in Haiti, he began a propaganda campaign in the rural areas of Spanish Santo Domingo to rouse the population to support the eventual annexation of the Spanish colony to Haiti. Knowing that the public was on his side, Boyer easily walked into Santo Domingo in early 1822, finally abolishing slavery in the colony. The Republic of Haiti thus controlled all of Hispaniola just four years after Boyer's coming to power.

Boyer's Haiti

The unification of Haiti under President Boyer marked a new beginning in the nation's history. Many were hopeful that the young country could make an economic comeback, something that would dramatically change the lives of its population for the better. Nevertheless, Haiti still had to face many problems, and international recognition of the nation was still up in the air. Haiti's ports traded with independent Spanish, British, and French merchants, but all these powers had been wary of recognizing Haiti as an independent nation.

In France, as we mentioned earlier, many were confident of Haiti's eventual return to the colonial Saint-Domingue that would supply Paris with important goods such as sugar and coffee. However, as Boyer ended the internal conflict within Haiti and annexed Santo Domingo, it became clear that hopes of reestablishing French colonial control over the new nation were unrealistic.

This was not only due to Boyer's victories and the trust the Haitian population seemingly expressed in their leader. The American world was rapidly changing in the early nineteenth century. Many Spanish colonies in Latin America had revolted against the Spanish Crown, as well, in 1808 as Napoleon invaded Iberia. Though the Spanish Crown would resist Napoleon's invasion and come back to power in 1814, by then, many Latin American independence movements had become far too pressing to ignore.

It is unclear to what extent Haitian independence had influenced these movements, but Simon Bolivar, the main figure in Latin American revolutions, had taken refuge in Pétion's republic in 1816. It was in Haiti where Bolivar's anti-slavery sentiments were reconfirmed.

Jean-Pierre Boyer, unknown painter.
https://commons.wikimedia.org/wiki/File:President_Jean-Pierre_Boyer_of_Haiti_(Hispaniola_Unification_Regime)_Portrait.jpg

The American Monroe Doctrine was another reason the prospect of France's return to Haiti seemed more unrealistic. The young American republic, viewing itself as a future great power of the New World, believed that the colonial age in the Western Hemisphere was over for Europeans. The Monroe Doctrine, advocated for by President James Monroe and issued right as the Latin American independence movements were becoming more prominent, proclaimed that the US would firmly oppose the establishment of any new European colonial presence in the Americas. This was done to ensure that the US would emerge as a dominant power in the West at the expense of the British, French, or Spanish presence.

The assertion of the Monroe Doctrine and the overall revolutionary spirit in the New World meant that the restoration government in France was in no position to return to Haiti as colonial overlords. In addition, the restored Bourbon monarchy had to address the overall instability that had characterized France since the beginning of the French Revolution in 1789 and persisted through Napoleon's empire.

Thus, in 1825, the French government changed its approach with Haiti and opened negotiations about the potential recognition of Haitian independence. Boyer acknowledged the importance that this would have for his republic and was ready to speak with the French representatives who arrived in Haiti in the spring of 1825.

The French demands were brutal. Paris demanded that a reparation payment of 150 million francs be paid to the former colonists who had suffered economically throughout the revolution since 1791. Haiti was also to reduce tariffs on imported French goods by half. The French delegation, which arrived with a small naval squadron, made it clear to President Boyer that this was more of an ultimatum than a proposal. The demands for reparation payments came as a part of a wider policy of the restoration government, which sought to reimburse the property losses of the French nobility during the revolution. The powerful lobby of former colonists from Saint-Domingue had put pressure on the French government to also provide compensation for them. France, still in a deep economic crisis, could not afford to satisfy the demands of the former colonists, whose interests and security it had failed to defend.

Though the terms of the "agreement" were too harsh on Haiti, Boyer was ready to pay a price for international recognition of his republic, still hopeful that future economic growth would make the payment of 150 million francs to France easier as time went by. He also may have hoped to later renegotiate the terms. To cover the costs, the French government brokered a deal for a loan between Boyer and French banks.

Despite his best hopes, however, Boyer had overestimated the prospect of his nation's economic recovery. By 1825, the flow of trade had been disturbed way too much. Though Haiti had at one time been the best producer of coffee and sugar, it was no longer able to keep up with better competition. Production of sugar and coffee had been advanced and adopted on a large scale in places such as Jamaica, Cuba, and Brazil, whose stable domestic conditions allowed for a steady production of these goods. The appearance of competitors resulted in an overall drop in coffee prices, which had adverse effects on the already struggling Haitian population. These factors led to Haiti defaulting on its loans soon after they were taken out from the French banks.

In the following years, as Haiti struggled to keep up its payments, the French government considered many options to force the young nation to pay. But it could not enforce its demands. France always had something more immediate on its agenda to deal with, such as the return of revolutionary sentiments and new endeavors in colonizing Algeria. In 1838, the two nations thus revised the agreement of 1825, giving Haiti more breathing room that allowed it to pay yearly reparations. This year thus marked France's official recognition of Haiti, though all the indemnities would not be paid off until 1893.

Boyer's presidency was unable to change the fundamental issues that were present in Haiti in the early nineteenth century. For ordinary Haitians, their new president for life was just another on the list of authoritarian rulers. His government was much like the dictatorial governments of Dessalines, Toussaint, Christophe, and Pétion, though Boyer's rule was marked by a long period of relative political stability. The president's authority largely depended on his relationship with the army, which he used to enforce even stricter labor regulations, intensifying the divide between Haiti's urban and rural populations. It became clear that, fundamentally, there was no difference between Boyer and his predecessors.

Nevertheless, on paper, the young Haitian Republic was one of the most progressive countries in the world. While major powers of Europe such as Russia or Austria lacked constitutional documents that clearly defined rights for their citizens, Haiti had managed to build the first black republic. It also had an advanced criminal code, which was largely adopted from Napoleonic France. Though Boyer's measures did not lead to the expected economic growth based on the factors mentioned, the new Haitian society, dominated by the descendants of the former slaves of Saint-Domingue, began to show its unique nature. By the mid-nineteenth century, it had a distinctive culture and a bustling social structure that at least tried to uphold the principles of egalitarianism. Compared to other places in the Caribbean where slavery was still practiced, Haiti was by all means a prosperous nation.

Boyer was overthrown in 1843, ending his almost twenty-five-year tenure as president. The revolt was instigated by a group of liberal reformers who protested Boyer's authoritarian military dictatorship and announced a new constitution. However, they would fail to maintain their influence and be overthrown by a military coup four years later when Faustin Soulouque, a former slave and participant in the original 1791 uprising, established his rule over Haiti.

In the 1840s, the Spanish part of Hispaniola also revolted against Haiti and broke away as the independent Dominican Republic. Haitian rulers would try to reimpose their control over the former colony of Santo Domingo but to no avail. In the end, the borders of the Republic of Haiti were reduced to their pre-1822 status.

Conclusion

The history of the Haitian Revolution is unique for many reasons. In 1791, at the time of the two unconnected uprisings in the French colony of Saint-Domingue, nobody would have expected that in fifteen years, the colony would become an independent republic with a president and a constitution that guaranteed equal rights for all male citizens regardless of their skin color. In Europe and the New World of the eighteenth century, imagining the complete abolition of slavery and the establishment of a completely non-white government in a former colony was very difficult.

The United States, the first major colony that had escaped European domination, was in all aspects, much more European than Haiti. At the time of the American Revolution, the fight was led by the majority white colonial population, unlike in Haiti where the black slave population significantly outnumbered the white colonists. The two revolutions are often compared because they are the two earliest examples of a successful revolt against European powers who had taken control of their territories for granted and resorted to the exploitation of colonial populations. Even when compared to other Caribbean or Latin American societies of the time, Haiti was very different. Nowhere else had the slave economy been so developed as in Haiti and a colony been so profitable and valuable as it had been.

French Saint-Domingue had been, indeed, the Pearl of the Antilles. And many hoped, throughout the Haitian Revolution until the declaration of independence in 1804 and beyond, that independent

Haiti would continue its role as a dominant exporter of the most important commodities at the time—sugar and coffee. However, due to a series of unpredictable personalities that used their power to continue to exploit most of the population and complexities in the international political climate, Haiti never reached its full potential.

One reason for this was the inexperience of the former slave population with self-governance or even independent livelihood. When the uprisings broke out, the objectives of the black population were ill-defined. Even when the movement grew and gained more attention from international actors, Haitians could not decide what was best for them. The influence of France and its revolution played a massive role in this regard. The Haitian revolutionaries tried to at first blindly follow the revolutionary spirit of Paris, believing it would bring an end to their exploitation. They were incorrect in assuming, however, that France would allow its most prized possession to slip out of its control so easily. And, as the revolutionary movement in Haiti achieved more success, its leaders began to use their power to leverage more concessions from the colonial regime, only after which were they ready to defy their rule.

It is perhaps difficult to properly put into words the impact of the Haitian Revolution. It not only influenced ongoing international political events but also fundamentally challenged the preconceived notions held by the European civilization about the nature of slavery and racial differences. When Haitians declared their independence in 1804, Europeans, first the French and later others, were forced to question whether their imposition of a "superior civilization" on the people they had believed to be inferior was valid.

Though sentiments about the abolition of slavery and even potential equality between white and black people had been expressed before and during the French Revolution, after the events in Haiti, the world had to confront these very pressing issues. In the United States, the question would be decided in the 1860s with the American Civil War that ended the practice of slavery. For Europe of the nineteenth century, however, the loss of long-standing colonial possessions in the New World and the resulting self-governance of non-white populations produced different effects. Europeans, hungry to dominate the world and justifying their colonial endeavors by claiming they were bringing civilization to underdeveloped areas, turned their attention to new horizons ripe for exploitation.

In fact, the era of European imperialism reached its peak in the latter half of the nineteenth century, as European superpowers sought to divide Africa, India, East Asia, and Oceania into their spheres of influence. The European colonial presence in these places was only different from slavery in everything but name, and the scale of the atrocities committed based on racial segregation would overshadow even those of the Haitian Revolution, which had become notorious for the massacre of white people by the black dictators of Haiti.

Although Europeans, led by the British, proceeded to officially ban the African slave trade in the years immediately following the Haitian Revolution, many were fearful that the disruption in this elaborate system would bring economic disadvantages. For example, Portugal notoriously continued the African slave trade into its South American colony of Brazil throughout the nineteenth century.

Still, as descendants of African slaves from other parts of the world looked up to Haiti's example, no other slave rebellion would end with the same success as the one in Haiti. The importance of the Haitian Revolution and the unique precedent it set in 1804 would only be properly acknowledged during the post-war period in the latter half of the twentieth century. The end of World War II marked a period of decolonization around the world.

The twentieth-century independence movements in African nations certainly could have learned the most from the example of Haiti. Many nations would also suffer similar fates. The main problem was not defeating the colonizers. (Though in some places, like in French Algeria, brutal fighting between the French colonists and Algerian nationalists would last for many years and cost the lives of hundreds of thousands of people.) A more pressing issue was what to do after decolonization. In many African nations that gained their independence in the post-war period of the twentieth century, the defeat of the colonists did not bring an overall improvement in living conditions, just like in Haiti. In these countries, the effects of European exploitation, years of fighting for independence, and domestic and external conflicts that followed decolonization are still clearly visible in the twenty-first century.

It is also interesting to examine the memory of the Haitian Revolution in the eyes of Haitians themselves. Interestingly, for the outside world, the person most associated with the revolution is Toussaint Louverture, and for good reason. In Haiti, however, it is Jean-Jacques Dessalines.

This is strange when we consider the fact that, at the time of his assassination, Dessalines was a very unpopular figure whose body was violently desecrated by the public. Haitians are most aware of the crimes committed by the infamously brutal general-turned-emperor and his reign of terror.

Attitudes towards Dessalines began to change, however, after the mid-nineteenth century. Dessalines is now an *Iwa,* a spirit in the vodou pantheon. Haitians especially commend him for his defeat of the French and assertion of independence, which Toussaint unable to do when he was in power. The former Haitian emperor has a lot of statues and memorials dedicated to him throughout the country, and Haiti's anthem, "La Dessalinienne," composed in the twentieth century, alludes to the egalitarian principles he aimed to uphold.

In conclusion, the story of the Haitian Revolution is complex and unique. It set many important precedents that opened up new avenues for oppressed people around the world. Most importantly, it all came at a terrible cost, the effects of which can still be observed in the country today. Tens of thousands died from 1791 to 1804, and many more in the years immediately following the proclamation of independence. In fact, the Haitian Revolution is infamous for its brutality, partly due to the atrocious images created by the French, who sometimes exaggerated their accounts of the uprisings. Still, it remains an inspiring story of the fight for liberation. Perhaps it is not fair to mention it only as part of the Atlantic revolutions of the late eighteenth century, though there are certainly many similarities between the three movements. Instead, the remarkability of the Haitian Revolution lies in the fact that it achieved something unprecedented and unimaginable. Above all, its main legacy is that it challenged existing paradigms about human nature, about what a particular group is and can do if they have clear goals and, more importantly, strength of mind.

If you enjoyed this book, a review on Amazon would be greatly appreciated because it would mean a lot to hear from you.

To leave a review:

1. Open your camera app.
2. Point your mobile device at the QR code.
3. The review page will appear in your web browser.

Thanks for your support!

Here's another book by Enthralling History that you might like

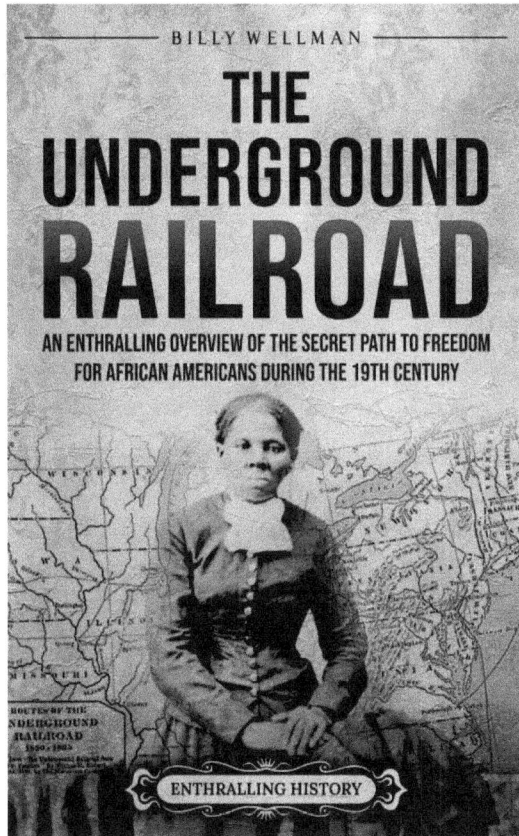

BILLY WELLMAN

THE UNDERGROUND RAILROAD

AN ENTHRALLING OVERVIEW OF THE SECRET PATH TO FREEDOM FOR AFRICAN AMERICANS DURING THE 19TH CENTURY

ENTHRALLING HISTORY

Free limited time bonus

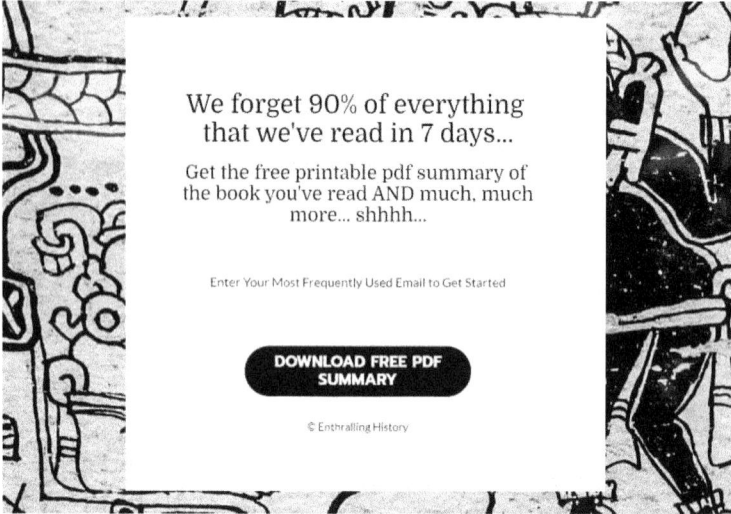

We forget 90% of everything that we've read in 7 days...

Get the free printable pdf summary of the book you've read AND much, much more... shhhh...

Enter Your Most Frequently Used Email to Get Started

DOWNLOAD FREE PDF SUMMARY

© Enthralling History

Stop for a moment. We have a free bonus set up for you. The problem is this: we forget 90% of everything that we read after 7 days. Crazy fact, right? Here's the solution: we've created a printable, 1-page pdf summary for this book that you're reading now. All you have to do to get your free pdf summary is to go to the following website: **https://livetolearn.lpages.co/enthrallinghistory/**

Or, Scan the QR code!

Once you do, it will be intuitive. Enjoy, and thank you!

Sources

1. Baur, J. E. (1947). Mulatto Machiavelli, Jean Pierre Boyer, and The Haiti of His Day. *The Journal of Negro History, 32*(3), 307-353. https://doi.org/10.2307/2715230

2. Destin, Y. (2014). Haiti's Prized Presidential Legacies. *Journal of Haitian Studies, 20*(2), 191-207. http://www.jstor.org/stable/24340374

3. Fischer, S. (2016). Inhabiting Rights. *L'Esprit Créateur, 56*(1), 52-67. https://www.jstor.org/stable/26378108

4. Gaffield, J. (2007). Complexities of Imagining Haiti: A Study of National Constitutions, 1801-1807. *Journal of Social History, 41*(1), 81-103. http://www.jstor.org/stable/25096441

5. Ghachem, M. W. (2003). Introduction: Slavery and Citizenship in the Age of the Atlantic Revolutions. *Historical Reflections / Réflexions Historiques, 29*(1), 7-17. http://www.jstor.org/stable/41299257

6. Knight, F. W. (2000). The Haitian Revolution. *The American Historical Review, 105*(1), 103-115. https://doi.org/10.2307/2652438

7. Ott, T. O. (1987). *The Haitian Revolution, 1789-1804*. Univ. of Tennessee Press.

8. Peguero, V. (1998). Teaching the Haitian Revolution: Its Place in Western and Modern World History. *The History Teacher, 32*(1), 33-41. https://doi.org/10.2307/494418

9. Popkin, J. D. (2021). *A concise history of the Haitian Revolution*. John Wiley & Sons.

10. Thomson, J. (2000). The Haitian Revolution and the Forging of America. *The History Teacher, 34*(1), 76–94. http://www.jstor.org/stable/3054377

www.ingramcontent.com/pod-product-compliance
Lightning Source LLC
LaVergne TN
LVHW051754080426
835511LV00018B/3315